WILMA RUDOLPH

Recent Titles in Greenwood Biographies

Bill Russell: A Biography
Murry R. Nelson

Venus and Serena Williams: A Biography
Jacqueline Edmondson

Flannery O'Connor: A Biography
Melissa Simpson

Jane Goodall: A Biography
Meg Greene

The Leakeys: A Biography
Mary Bowman-Kruhm

Arthur Ashe: A Biography
Richard Steins

Cesar Chavez: A Biography
Roger Bruns

F. Scott Fitzgerald: A Biography
Edward J. Rielly

Saddam Hussein: A Biography
Shiva Balaghi

Tiger Woods: A Biography
Lawrence J. Londino

Mohandas K. Gandhi: A Biography
Patricia Cronin Marcello

Muhammad Ali: A Biography
Anthony O. Edmonds

Martin Luther King, Jr.: A Biography
Roger Bruns

WILMA RUDOLPH

A Biography

Maureen M. Smith

GREENWOOD BIOGRAPHIES

GREENWOOD PRESS
WESTPORT, CONNECTICUT · LONDON

Library of Congress Cataloging-in-Publication Data

Smith, Maureen M.
    Wilma Rudolph : a biography / Maureen Smith.
        p. cm.—(Greenwood biographies, ISSN 1540–4900)
    Includes bibliographical references and index.
    ISBN 0–313–33307–6
    1. Rudolph, Wilma, 1940– 2. Runners (Sports)—United States—Biography.
3. Women runners—United States—Biography. I. Title. II. Series.
GV1061.15.R83S64   2006
796.42092—dc22   2006007007

British Library Cataloguing in Publication Data is available.

This book is included in the African American Experience database from Greenwood
Electronic Media. For more information, visit www.africanamericanexperience.com.

Library of Congress Catalog Card Number: 2006007007
ISBN: 0–313–33307–6
ISSN: 1540–4900

First published in 2006

Greenwood Press, 88 Post Road West, Westport, CT 06881
An imprint of Greenwood Publishing Group, Inc.
www.greenwood.com

Printed in the United States of America

The paper used in this book complies with the
Permanent Paper Standard issued by the National
Information Standards Organization (Z39.48–1984).

10 9 8 7 6 5 4 3 2 1

This book is dedicated to the memory of Wilma Rudolph, an American and Olympic icon; she ran fast decades before such talent was appreciated by the American public. Despite the obstacles, Wilma approached life with grace, courage, and determination. This book is dedicated to the Tennessee State University Tigerbelles, past, present, and future. This book is dedicated to my two nieces, Zoe and Nell—may they love running and reading.

CONTENTS

Series Foreword   ix

Acknowledgments   xi

Introduction: African American Women in Sport   xiii

Timeline: Significant Events in Wilma Rudolph's Life   xxi

Chapter 1 A Legend is Born—The Early Days of Wilma Rudolph   1

Chapter 2 Wilma Removes the Leg Braces and Gets Involved in
Athletics   7

Chapter 3 Meeting Ed Temple and Running with the
Tennessee State Tigerbelles   15

Chapter 4 Running at the 1956 Olympic Games   29

Chapter 5 Coming Home to Burt High School   41

Chapter 6 Becoming a Tennessee State Tigerbelle   47

Chapter 7 Wilma Runs to History at the 1960 Olympic Games   55

Chapter 8 Wilma's Post-Olympic Competitions   67

Chapter 9 Wilma Rudolph: An American Image   77

Chapter 10 Hanging Up the Spikes: Wilma in Retirement   85

Chapter 11 Wilma on Wilma—Writing Her Own Story   95

Chapter 12 The Legacy of Wilma Rudolph—From Evelyn
Ashford to Marion Jones   103

Appendix: Performances of African
      American Women
       in Olympic Track and Field   113

Bibliography   127

Index   131

Photo essay follows page 54

SERIES FOREWORD

In response to high school and public library needs, Greenwood developed this distinguished series of full-length biographies specifically for student use. Prepared by field experts and professionals, these engaging biographies are tailored for high school students who need challenging yet accessible biographies. Ideal for secondary school assignments, the length, format, and subject areas are designed to meet educators' requirements and students' interests.

Greenwood offers an extensive selection of biographies spanning all curriculum related subject areas including social studies, the sciences, literature and the arts, history and politics, as well as popular culture, covering public figures and famous personalities from all time periods and backgrounds, both historic and contemporary, who have made an impact on American and world culture. Greenwood biographies were chosen based on comprehensive feedback from librarians and educators. Consideration was given to both curriculum relevance and inherent interest. The result is an intriguing mix of the well known and the unexpected, the saints and sinners from long-ago history and contemporary pop culture. Readers will find a wide array of subject choices from fascinating crime figures like Al Capone to inspiring pioneers like Margaret Mead, from the greatest minds of our time like Stephen Hawking to the most amazing success stories of our day like J. K. Rowling.

While the emphasis is on fact, not glorification, the books are meant to be fun to read. Each volume provides in-depth information about the subject's life from birth through childhood, the teen years, and adulthood. A thorough account relates family background and education, traces personal and professional influences, and explores struggles, accomplish-ments, and contributions. A timeline highlights the most significant life events against a historical perspective. Bibliographies supplement the reference value of each volume.

ACKNOWLEDGMENTS

I would like to acknowledge the assistance I received from Steven Vetrano and Catherine Piorkowski of Greenwood Publishing, as well as the editorial input received from Katie Landmark, which proved extremely invaluable. The Sacramento State Archives staff was helpful in locating the available materials on Wilma Rudolph's short employment at the school. I greatly appreciate the feedback provided by Ellen Carlton, who read this manuscript several times and was willing to talk about Wilma Rudolph with me more times than I can remember.

INTRODUCTION: AFRICAN AMERICAN WOMEN IN SPORT

To be a woman in such an age carries with it a privilege and an opportunity never implied before. But to be a woman of the Negro race in America, and to be able to grasp the deep significance of the possibilities of the crisis, is to have a heritage, it seems to me, unique in the ages.[1]

—Anna Julia Cooper

Following the end of slavery in the United States, Anna Julia Cooper addressed the role of women in the achievement of national identity and American citizenship for Africans in America. Cooper was a leading advocate of women's rights, and her writings on gaining American citizenship were based upon the premise that only when Black women enjoyed the same rights as American citizens could any other American, Black or White, enjoy the same freedoms. Cooper wrote, "Only the Black Woman can say when and where I enter, in the quiet, undisputed dignity of my womanhood, without violence and without suing or special patronage, then and there the whole Negro race enters with me."[2] Bringing the issue of gender to the forefront, Cooper clearly recognized the need to gain full rights as American citizens, and foresaw this happening only when Black women were included and that only when Black women are afforded this full participation would the whole nation, Black and White, male and female, enjoy such freedoms.

One hundred years later, Cooper's aspirations and hope for Black females are still being realized. The sporting arena has emerged as a central stage for the accomplishments and achievements of Black females. African American women are disproportionately represented in two sports, basketball and track and field, though there are individual Black women making their name in other sports. Today, women's basketball offers professional opportunities for women in the United States with rosters dominated by Black females, such as Lisa Leslie, Sheryl Swoopes, Chamique Holdsclaw, Tameka Catchings, and Yolanda Griffith. Endorsements, magazine articles, and other commercial opportunities present America with a variety of images of successful athletic African American females. Beyond basketball, Black women are widely recognized in track and field, and more recently, with the rise of the Williams sisters, Serena and Venus, on the tennis court. On playing fields, tennis courts, in swimming pools, and at sport complexes, increasing numbers of Black females are competing in a wide range of sports, some famous, most in relative obscurity. Clearly, the implications of today's visible, and sometimes invisible, success of African American women is steeped in a history of Black women's participation in sport that is widely unknown and unrecognized.

The written history of African American women's participation in sport is mostly descriptive; lists of names, numbers, and events. Little analysis of their patterns of participation and the significance of their sporting activities has been completed. It has been noted that "with the possible exception of Wilma Rudolph and Althea Gibson, the great and near-great black female athletes have been fleetingly, if ever, in the consciousness of the sporting public. Nobody knows her: not publicists, nor researchers, nor entrepreneurs, nor published historians."[3] One could easily argue that even Gibson and Rudolph, who are often hailed as pioneers for African American women in integrated American sport, have only received minor attention in relation to their white sporting sisters. Contemporary scholars view this lack of attention on the accomplishments of Black female athletes as "a tragic loss for the American community, black and white, male and female," citing "the fact that the black American sportswoman has performed a prodigious psychological achievement.... To become a fine athlete she had to develop an assessment of herself in the face of a society which devalued her, as both a female and a black."[4] A brief mention of early African American female athletes is warranted here. African American female athletes in the twentieth century have a history, albeit an ignored one, that merits some discussion and further analysis. Ora Washington played basketball and tennis in the 1920s, 1930s, and 1940s. She won her first national tennis championship in 1924 and was the American Tennis

Association's national champion for seven years in a row (1929–1935). Washington was the captain of the YWCA Hornets basketball team in Germantown, Pennsylvania. She later joined the *Philadelphia Tribune* traveling squad.[5] Lucy Diggs Slowe, like Washington, also played tennis. She was the first African American Tennis Association women's singles champion in 1917. She was also the president of the Women's Tennis Club at Howard University, where she eventually became the first dean of women in 1922.[6] Toni Stone played on a number of semi-pro baseball teams, some integrated. She was the first woman to play in the Negro Leagues in 1953 with the Indianapolis Clowns.[7] Lula Mae Hymes captained the Tuskegee Institute track team from 1937 to 1939. She was also the Amateur Athletic Union (AAU) champion in both the long jump (1937 and 1938) and the 100-meter race (1939).[8] Betty Jean Lane was also a notable sprinter. Lane attended and competed for Wilberforce University in Ohio in the 1930s.[9] Ann Gregory was "the Queen of Negro Golf Women" according to the African American press. She dominated segregated golf and became the first Black woman to compete in United States Golf Association events.[10]

There were also teams that competed that deserve recognition. Wiggins suggests that the Tuskegee Institute track team was the "most famous group of African American women athletes" during the first half of the twentieth century. The team dominated AAU track championships in the 1930s and 1940s, winning 10 titles in 11 years (between 1937 and 1948).[11] Liberti chronicles the women's basketball team at Bennett College, a historically black college, between 1928 and 1942.[12] Leading up to the emergence of Gibson and Rudolph in the 1950s and 1960s, their sporting mothers competed primarily against segregated opponents and received little to no media coverage beyond their local boundaries. Many of their stories remain untold.

In examining the sporting accomplishments and participation of Black female women, it is important and not the least bit ironic that these female athletes, with all their talent, strength, and success as American athletes, eventually became just that—American athletes. Boxer Joe Louis and sprinter Jesse Owens played similar roles in the symbolic transition from being a Negro athlete to becoming an American athlete when they defeated Nazi opponents and Hitler's beliefs about Aryan supremacy in the 1930s. Owens won four gold medals at the 1936 Olympic Games hosted by Nazi leader Adolf Hitler in Berlin, Germany. Louis claimed his "American" status when he knocked out German Max Schmeling in 1938, who to most Americans represented Hitler's Nazi ideology. Both Owens and Louis became accepted as "Americans" with their sporting victories, with Blacks and Whites cheering them in their pursuit of Hitler's evil empire.[13]

It was the sporting successes of African American female athletes against the Soviet Union in the late 1950s and early 1960s that came to represent America in the Cold War athletic competitions. While their Black male counterparts emerged during the 1960s with a race consciousness exhibited through a number of boycott movements and other protests, Black female athletes were virtually deracinated by the sporting press and public battling both race and gender stereotypes. Moreover, the sporting accomplishments of Black female athletes were further minimized by a sporting public both as a result of their gender, as well as the public's general attitudes about gender. It is the gender stereotypes that are most apparent in the press coverage and discussion of the achievements of the Black female athletes during this time period, with few references being made to the skin color of the female athlete, with the coverage of Wilma Rudolph being a notable exception.

Scholar Carole Oglesby cites the "socio-economic and psychological milieu of the United States" as not being "conducive to the development of the black sportswoman" in the second half of the twentieth century. Oglesby sees the success of Black female athletes as indicative of their strength and perseverance. "That many have emerged on spite of this state of affairs is a great tribute to their human spirit and talent. We must look at the barriers in society to the development of the black sportswoman."[14] These barriers included The Moynihan Report, written in the 1960s and based partially on Franklin Frazier's writing on the disorganization of the black family. The report linked the "data on marital dissolution, illegitimacy rates, female-headed families and welfare dependency" to the breakdown of black families and wrote that "black women became scapegoats, responsible for the psychological emasculation of black men and the failure of the black community to gain parity with the white community."[15] The barrier wasn't the break down of the Black family, but the perceptions of the issue. The strength of Black women struggling to keep their families together, instead of being praised, was viewed as a disruptive strength. The strength of Black women was overlooked and disrespected in society and in sport. Moreover, Oglesby notes "African American women are among the lowest paid, the most undereducated, and most likely to receive public assistance, although proportionately more have always worked outside the home and been forced to develop mental and physical strength to resist daily dehumanization."[16] Sport sociologist Yevonne Smith writes that "despite their personal strength and integrity, women of color have historically been oppressed and omitted from the mainstream of society, sport, and scholarship."[17]

Wilma Rudolph was part of the first generation of African American women track stars who emerged at the 1960 Olympic Games, but who had been gaining ground in the U.S.–U.S.S.R. track and field meets in the years leading up to the Games. Wilma's story is one that is unmatched in both courage and determination. Born into a poor African American family in the segregated south, the odds were already stacked against Wilma. As a youth, she was plagued with a number of illnesses, including scarlet fever, pneumonia, whooping cough, and polio. The polio left her partially paralyzed and unable to walk without a brace until she was 11 years old. Once she removed the brace and was walking, she never stopped. Wilma started her athletic career by sitting on the bench of her basketball team for three years before becoming a starter on a championship team at Burt High School. She ran track and was invited to run at Coach Ed Temple's summer program at Tennessee State University in Nashville, Tennessee. She was the youngest member of the 1956 U.S. Olympic women's track team, where she won a bronze medal on the 400-meter relay. After graduating from high school, Wilma enrolled at Tennessee State and became one of Coach Temple's Tigerbelles, a team that dominated American women's track in the 1950s and 1960s. Wilma qualified for the 1960 Olympic Games in Rome, Italy, and at the Games won gold medals in the 100-meter and 200-meter dashes, and 4x100-meter relay, becoming the first American woman to win three gold medals in track and field. Quite an accomplishment for someone who had struggled to walk as a girl!

Despite her success on the track, Wilma struggled after she graduated from college and her track and field career was over. There were no commercial endorsements or professional contracts for female athletes. She bounced from job to job, and faced racism and sexism on a regular basis. She was valued for her Olympic victories by multiple organizations, but often disregarded for any contributions she might be able to make to such organizations. Despite the hardships Wilma Rudolph faced throughout her life, which included poverty, illness, racism, sexism, teen pregnancy, and two marriages, she refused to wallow in pity for her struggles. In her autobiography, *Wilma*, Wilma writes an account of her life that reveals an individual who chose to not reflect too deeply on the negative experiences, instead focusing on the successful details of her life.

One should assume that Wilma had to deal with racism and sexism which undoubtedly influenced her. She grew up during a time in America when the Jim Crow laws forced most Black Americans into the backs of buses, segregated classrooms, hotels, and restaurants. Women, too, faced expectations that questioned their femininity when they worked outside of the home, something many African American women did to help provide for their families. Still, Wilma makes little reference to her own encounters with racism, and writes almost nothing related to experiences with sexism and what it was like to compete as a female in a male dominated arena. One must certainly consider the times in which she was writing and the audience she hoped to reach. One must also bear in mind that her image was built solidly on a narrative about triumph, about overcoming odds, and ultimately about coming out on top. To address racism and sexism, or to even include incidents where she was not able to emerge victorious, simply would not have been consistent with the public persona of Wilma Rudolph. Despite her reluctance to share such failures, her autobiography offers readers a point from which to consider her remarkable achievements. Moreover, beyond a few books written for young readers, it is the only biographical account of her life.

Wilma Rudolph's story is more than the races she won and world records she established. It is the story of a young woman who overcame tremendous obstacles that should have kept her from ever experiencing athletic success, and yet she is the epitome of triumph. Her story is one of a kind.

NOTES

1. Anna Julia Cooper, *A Voice from the South* (New York: Negro Universities Press, 1969), 144. Cooper's book was originally published in 1892.

2. Cooper, *A Voice from the South,* 31.

3. Carole A. Oglesby, "Myths and Realities of Black Women in Sport," in *Black Women in Sport,* ed. Tina Sloan Green (Reston, VA: AAHPERD Publications, 1981), 1.

4. Oglesby, "Myths and Realities," 1.

5. Rita Liberti, "Ora Washington," in *African Americans in Sport: Volume 2,* ed. David K. Wiggins (Armonk, N.Y.: M.E. Sharpe, 2004), 391.

6. Doris R. Corbett, "Lucy Stowe Diggs," in *African Americans in Sport: Volume 2,* ed. David K. Wiggins (Armonk, N.Y.: M.E. Sharpe, 2004), 334.

7. Gai Ingham Berlage, "Toni Stone," in *African Americans in Sport: Volume 2,* ed. David K. Wiggins (Armonk, N.Y.: M.E. Sharpe, 2004), 349.

8. Alison M. Wrynn, "Lula Mae Hymes," in *African Americans in Sport: Volume 1,* ed. David K. Wiggins (Armonk, N.Y.: M.E. Sharpe, 2004), 162.

9. Sara B. Washington, "Betty Jean Lane," in *African Americans in Sport: Volume 1,* ed. David K. Wiggins (Armonk, N.Y.: M.E. Sharpe, 2004), 200.

10. Calvin H. Sinnette, "Ann Gregory," in *African Americans in Sport: Volume 1*, ed. David K. Wiggins (Armonk, N.Y.: M.E. Sharpe, 2004), 130.

11. David K. Wiggins, "Women," in *African Americans in Sport: Volume 2*, ed. David K. Wiggins (Armonk, N.Y.: M.E. Sharpe, 2004), 414.

12. Rita M. Liberti, " 'We Were Ladies, We Just Played Basketball Like Boys' African American Womanhood and Competitive Basketball at Bennett College, 1928–1942," *Journal of Sport History*, 26 (Fall 1999): 567–84.

13. For an excellent account of the 1936 Olympic Games, see Richard D. Mandell, *The Nazi Olympics* (Urbana: University of Illinois Press, 1987).

14. Oglesby, "Myths and Realities," 2.

15. Oglesby, "Myths and Realities," 8.

16. Yevonne R. Smith, "Women of Color in Society and Sport," *Quest* (August 1992), 235.

17. Smith, "Women of Color," 231.

TIMELINE: SIGNIFICANT EVENTS IN WILMA RUDOLPH'S LIFE

June 23, 1940	Wilma Glodean Rudolph is born in St. Bethelem, Tennessee.
1952	Wilma is able to walk without the aid of leg braces or crutches and, upon entering junior high, begins playing basketball on the Burt High School girls team.
Summer 1955	Wilma attends the summer training program with Coach Ed Temple at Tennessee State University. She competes in her first Amateur Athletic Union (AAU) championship track meet.
Summer 1956	Wilma is victorious at her second AAU meet and qualifies for the Olympic Trials. She qualifies for the 1956 Olympic track and field team and wins a bronze medal at the Olympic Games in Melbourne, Australia.
May 1958	Wilma graduates from Burt High School in Clarksville, Tennessee.
July 1958	Wilma gives birth to her first daughter, Yolanda. Yolanda's father is Wilma's high school boyfriend, Roger Eldridge.
Fall 1958	Wilma starts college at Tennessee State University. She is a member of the women's track and field team, the Tigerbelles.

September 1960   Wilma becomes the first American woman
                        to win three Olympic gold medals in track
                        and field at the Olympic Games. She wins the
                        medals in the 100- and 200-meter dashes and
                        the 4 x 100-meter relay.
Awards won in 1960   Associated Press Female Athlete of the
                        Year; Christopher Columbus Award (Italy);
                        Helms World Trophy for North America; *Los
                        Angeles Times* Award for women's track and
                        field; European Sportswriters Association Out-
                        standing Athlete of the Year; Mademoiselle's
                        Outstanding Achievement Award; *New York
                        Times* Outstanding Women in the U.S. Award;
                        Sports Magazine Award as top performer in track
                        and field; *Nashville Banner* Outstanding Athlete
                        of the Year; National Newspaper Publishers
                        Association's Russwurm Award; Babe Didrikson
                        Zaharias Award for outstanding American
                        female athlete.
October 14, 1961   Wilma marries fellow Tennessee State student,
                        William Ward.
Awards won in 1961   Associated Press Female Athlete of the Year;
                        Sullivan Award as top U.S. amateur athlete.
1962   Wilma divorces William Ward.
May 1963   Wilma graduates from college with a degree in
                        elementary education.
Summer 1963   Wilma marries her high school sweetheart,
                        Robert Eldridge.
1964   Wilma and Robert welcome their second child,
                        Djuana, a daughter.
1965   Wilma and Robert's third child, and first son,
                        Robert, Jr. is born.
1971   Wilma and Robert's fourth child, and second
                        son, Xurry is born.
1973   Wilma is inducted into the Black Sports Hall of
                        Fame.
1974   Wilma is inducted into the U.S. Track and
                        Field Hall of Fame.
1977   Wilma writes her autobiography, *Wilma: The
                        Story of Wilma Rudolph*, which is made into a
                        television movie.

1980	Wilma divorces Robert Eldridge; Wilma is inducted into the National Women's Hall of Fame.
1981	Wilma starts the Wilma Rudolph Foundation.
1983	Wilma is inducted into the Tennessee State University Hall of Fame and the U.S. Olympic Hall of Fame.
1990	Wilma receives the NCAA Silver Anniversary Award.
1991	Wilma is given the Crown Royal Achievement Award.
June 1993	Wilma is honored by American President Bill Clinton at the first National Sports Awards.
1994	Wilma wins the National Woman's Hall of Fame Award; a section of Route 79 in Clarksville is renamed Wilma Rudolph Boulevard; she was awarded two honorary degrees.
November 12, 1994	Wilma Rudolph dies of brain cancer in Brentwood, Tennessee.
August 11, 1995	Tennessee State University dedicates their new dormitory facility as the Wilma G. Rudolph Residence Center.
June 23, 1997	Tennessee Governor Don Sundquist proclaims June 23rd (Wilma's birthday) to be Wilma Rudolph Day in Tennessee.
1999	Wilma is ranked number 41 by ESPN in their list of the twentieth century's greatest athletes.
2004	The U.S. Postal Service unveils a postal stamp of Wilma Rudolph as part of their Distinguished American Series.

Chapter 1

A LEGEND IS BORN—
THE EARLY DAYS
OF WILMA RUDOLPH

Wilma Glodean Rudolph entered this world on June 23, 1940, two months premature after her mother experienced a fall. As a tiny infant, she weighed only four and a half pounds. Few would have guessed on that fateful day in St. Bethelem, Tennessee, that the small, fragile little girl would become one of the world's greatest sprinters. The 20th of her father's 22 children, Wilma was born into a family that struggled with poverty, but according to Wilma, made up for it with love for each other.[1] Many of her older brothers and sisters were already adults and no longer living in the Rudolph home. Her father, Ed Rudolph, was a railroad porter, and her mother, Blanche, worked as a domestic for White families. Neither Rudolph parent had completed elementary school. Her mother could read and write, but her father could not. In her autobiography, Wilma recalled that her parents' annual income never amounted to more than $2,500.[2] Wilma's mother would make dresses for Wilma from old flour sacks because the family did not have enough money for clothes. They lived in a wooden frame house, common for Blacks in Clarksville, had no electricity, and the family used an outhouse. For lighting they used kerosene lamps and candles.

Wilma experienced many childhood illnesses as a result of her premature birth. As a very young child, Wilma developed polio and the illness left her with legs that were crippled and unable to run around like other children her age. She also suffered through double pneumonia, scarlet fever, measles, mumps, and whooping cough, all before her seventh birthday. Dr. Coleman was the Black doctor in town and treated all the Black families in Clarksville, which was common practice in the segregated

South. Dr. Coleman would tell her, "Wilma everything is gonna turn out all right. You just fight this thing, you understand?"[3] The height of the polio epidemic, also called poliomyelitis, came in 1952, just as Wilma was recovering from the debilitating virus. Caused by a filterable virus, polio was a highly contagious infectious disease. One common effect of the debilitating disease was paralysis and though it could strike at any age, it most often infected children. In 1952, there were 60,000 reported cases and 3,000 deaths from polio. A polio vaccination was created in 1955 by Dr. Jonas Salk, and the disease was eventually eliminated from the United States.

When Wilma was five, she started wearing a steel brace on her left leg.[4] Designed to keep her leg straight, she admitted years later that the brace always reminded her that something was wrong with her. She wrote that wearing the brace was psychologically devastating.[5] By the age of six, the home exercises she had been doing were not working to help her mobility, and her mother began taking her to Meharry Hospital, the Black medical college of Fisk University in Nashville, and 50 miles from Clarksville. She and her mother would take the Greyhound bus to Nashville where Wilma's leg would be stretched, pulled, and twisted. At that time, bus stations and buses were segregated, which meant that Wilma and her mother had to sit in the back of the bus and obey the racial practices in the bus stations, including restaurants and restrooms. Because of the segregation practices in the South, Wilma could not be treated at the local hospital in Clarksville. She commented that she could not remember a Black person ever challenging the rules of segregation on the bus and that the practice took its toll on the self-esteem of Black people.[6] Wilma felt that Black people of that era were fairly resigned to the system of Jim Crow and that their going along with the laws signaled their acceptance of the practice.

The doctors at Meharry told Mrs. Rudolph that if Wilma underwent heat and water therapy, along with therapeutic massages, she might be able to regain the use of her left leg. They would put her leg into a whirlpool that was very hot. When Wilma would return home from Meharry she would look at her leg to see if it was any better. She developed a walk she called the "fake no-limp" walk that made it seem like she was able to walk without a limp and lead her family, and herself, to believe that she was getting better. Her mother and brothers and sisters would all take turns massaging Wilma's legs four times a day and eventually she was able to walk with the aid of special orthopedic shoes. The one "fringe benefit" to Wilma's hospital treatments was that it excused her from doing any household chores. Her brothers did the heavy chores, such as cutting firewood, while her sisters would wash the dishes. She would entertain them as they cleaned and described herself as her siblings' "gimpy-legged cheerleader."[7] Wilma's memories of her childhood celebrated her family and the love they had for one another.

Wilma's childhood illnesses made attending school impossible and she was tutored at home by her mother. She missed all of kindergarten and first grade. With braces on her legs, Wilma was finally able to start walking and at the age of seven entered the second grade at Cobb Elementary. Cobb Elementary was the school for the African American children in Clarksville. Because it only served Black students, the school was poorly funded and often lacked adequate resources such as books, equipment, and teachers; another result of the social practices of racism in the segregated South. Wilma entered school several years before the 1954 Brown versus the Board of Education ruling that outlawed segregated education and established that separate schools for White and Black children did not produce equal education. Even though the Supreme Court ruling came while Wilma was enrolled in high school, she never experienced an integrated educational setting, as the schools in Clarksville, as in many American cities, did not desegregate for some years after the ruling.

Wilma felt lonely as a child because her illnesses not only kept her out of school, but also kept her inside and away from other children her age. Neighborhood children teased her, calling her "cripple,"[8] and never included her in their activities. As expected, her brothers and sisters defended her, but the exclusion still stung. Besides the loneliness, Wilma also reported she felt rejected. On her first day of school, she was terrified of both being in school and being with kids her own age. She sought to be accepted and recalls that on the outside she seemed happy for the first time in her life. Her first teacher was Mrs. Allison, who was also her Brownies troop leader. That first year in school, Wilma went from being the sickest kid in Clarksville to finally feeling some sense of being normal and accepted by other children her age, something that was priceless to the young girl.[9] Eventually, a competitive spirit in Wilma emerged which helped her to rehabilitate her legs as she was determined to be able to play with the other children and prove that she belonged.

Wilma confessed that "all of those years being sick left a lot of scars on me mentally. Those years left me very insecure. I was a sensitive person to begin with, and you combine sensitivity with insecurity and you've got some case on your hands ... I lived in mortal fear of being disliked."[10] When she was nine years old, Wilma took her brace off and walked into her church to the surprise of her fellow parishioners. Despite still having to go back and forth to Meharry for her treatment, Wilma recalled her walk into church as a big moment in her young life. It signaled to everyone, young and old, that she was more than the brace on her leg. "I went from being a sickly kid the other kids teased to a normal person accepted by my peer group, and that was the most important thing that could have happened to me at that point in my life. I needed to belong, and I finally did."[11] This insecurity would plague Wilma throughout her life despite the successes she later experienced.

Wilma stopped her treatments at Meharry when she was 10 and finally, by the time Wilma turned 12 years old, she could walk normally, without the aid of crutches, the leg brace, or corrective shoes. Her mother packed the brace and mailed it off to the hospital in Nashville. At the end of sixth grade, Wilma recalls that she was a confused, unhappy girl, who still did not know anything about sports and had never played on a team. But she was feeling healthy and alive. As she watched other kids on the basketball court, she began to think she might be able to play herself. She was also very excited to be entering a new school for junior high.

Many of Wilma's early ideas about race were a result of her living in Clarksville, the segregated South, and seeing her mother work as a domestic doing menial chores for White people. She remembered resenting that her mother had to work for White people and decided that she would never work for White people. She recalled in her autobiography that there was something not right about the ways things were in Clarksville. "White folks got all the luxury, and we black folks got all the dirty work."[12] Every year she and her siblings would sit across from the gates to the county fair at the Clarksville fairgrounds and watch the White people enter. By the early age of six, she realized that White people treated their horses better than they treated Black people.[13] When she confronted her parents about the racial inequities, they told her not to be bothered by it and to accept it as the way things were. Her mother would frequently tell her "Hold your tongue." Segregated practices certainly influenced Wilma's early ideas about the privileges and restrictions that were assigned according to one's skin color. Still, in recalling her early childhood, Wilma never dwelled on the daily experiences of contending with being Black in the segregated American South during a time period when racial practices were entrenched.

Wilma's light complexion also influenced her ideas about race. Her brother Wesley was very dark skinned, her father was pale, and among her siblings there were a rainbow of brown hues. People would ask her why she was walking with Wesley, not realizing that the dark skinned boy was her brother and that she was also Black! Her early ideas and exposure, or lack of exposure, to White people contributed to her developing a belief that all White people were "mean and evil."[14] Two of Wilma's older brothers served in segregated military units in World War II, and she remembered hearing them talk about the hypocrisy of the government asking them to fight for freedom overseas when they were treated so poorly at home.

Wilma did not give much thought as a youth to broader race relations in the United States, and her worldview on race was limited to segregated Clarksville, where 75 percent of her town was White. Landers Café was the only restaurant in Clarksville where Blacks could eat. Taught by Black teachers, she had what she called a "Negro history course" in elementary school that taught the students about Black heroes, such as Booker T. Washington and George Washington Carver, but failed to tell them about slavery and lynching. As an adult, Wilma looked back on her school experiences and felt that her teachers, like her parents, were trying to protect her from the harsh racial realities, but at a cost. She lamented that there was no excuse why she did not know about slavery until as late as sixth grade and thought for sure that her great-grandparents must have been slaves. She never discussed this possibility with her parents.

Despite her view that White people were mean and evil, and her experiences growing up in a town where skin color dictated social practices, there was one place that shifted Wilma's attitudes about race as she grew into a teenager. Unlike other public facilities that were segregated by Jim Crow laws, church was one public space that welcomed Blacks living in the South. The Rudolph family was strict Baptists and required their children to attend church every Sunday, though Mr. Rudolph did not always accompany the family to church services. Still, the family participated in the local Baptist church, and it was a place that provided Wilma with a foundation for her spiritual beliefs.

Wilma's childhood was the beginning of her remarkable triumphs, starting with her first footsteps at her church. Despite the poverty her family endured, segregated Clarksville, in many ways, provided a small and safe African American community that took care of each other, from medical needs to education. Wilma did not dwell on the shortcomings of her childhood, even if she did recognize that Jim Crow racial practices often restricted her community. Though she concedes that her illnesses had a profound effect on her sense of self, admitting that she felt lonely and insecure as a child, by the time Wilma entered junior high school without her leg brace, she found new opportunities that prove her to have been a resilient young woman. In almost every account of Wilma's amazing athletic achievements, her early childhood paralysis sets the story for her future triumphs.

NOTES

1. Wilma's father, Ed, already had 14 children when he married Wilma's mother, Blanche. Wilma was the sixth of eight children between Ed and Blanche Rudolph. See Bobby Lovett, "Leaders of Afro-American Nashville: Wilma Rudolph and the TSU Tigerbelles," 1997 Nashville Conference on Afro-American Culture and History. Located in Sacramento State University archives.

2. Wilma Rudolph, with Martin Ralbovsky, *Wilma: The Story of Wilma Rudolph* (New York: Signet, 1977), 5.

3. Rudolph, *Wilma*, 19.

4. Wayne Wilson, "Wilma Rudolph: The Making of an Olympic Icon," in *Sport and the Racial Mountain: A Biographical History of the African American Athlete*, ed. David K. Wiggins (Fayetteville: University of Arkansas Press, forthcoming). Wilson briefly addresses the discrepancies within Wilma's autobiography, including that at points in her book and in other sources, both legs are mentioned as being the afflicted leg.

5. Rudolph, *Wilma*, 29.

6. Rudolph, *Wilma*, 33–34.

7. Rudolph, *Wilma*, 37.

8. Rudolph, *Wilma*, 15.

9. Rudolph, *Wilma*, 21–22.

10. Rudolph, *Wilma*, 25–26.

11. Rudolph, *Wilma*, 22.

12. Rudolph, *Wilma*, 8.

13. Rudolph, *Wilma*, 7.

14. Rudolph, *Wilma*, 11.

Chapter 2

WILMA REMOVES
THE LEG BRACES AND GETS
INVOLVED IN ATHLETICS

After spending her young childhood in restrictive leg braces and corrective shoes, Wilma was eager to prove that she was not a sickly little girl. By the time she was 12, the leg brace was off, and Wilma was readying herself to enter junior high school. The summer before seventh grade, Wilma watched and played a lot of basketball at local playgrounds. Soon after, Wilma started playing basketball in the yard with her brothers. Initially Wilma's mother did not want her playing basketball, because she thought it would tire her out and she was still very protective of Wilma's health, though her father always allowed her to play. Her parents would sometimes argue about what types of physical activities Wilma should be allowed to do; only years earlier they had feared she would never be able to walk, much less play basketball. Playing sport was beyond any expectations and opened up a new world to Wilma. When she entered Burt High School, the newly built African American junior-senior high school named for Dr. Robert Tecumseh Burt, a Black physician, Wilma decided that she would try out for the girl's basketball team.[1] Her older sister Yvonne was already on the team.

Though she was a very small seventh grader, Wilma tried out for the team with the support of her parents who encouraged Yvonne to bring her younger sister along to the tryouts. Coach Clinton Gray kept young Wilma on the team, but she sat on the bench the entire season. Despite sitting on the bench, she learned a lot about the game as she studied the movement of all the players and prepared herself for when she might get into the game. She also learned that people had very strict ideas about what they thought was appropriate for girls to do—and many people believed that girls should not play basketball or any competitive sport.

In 1939, prominent Black physical educator Edwin Bancroft Henderson had agreed with other physical educators of the day that the "first priority of girls athletics should be health, not competition."[2] Competition was viewed as a masculine trait and inappropriate for females to engage in. However, Henderson also criticized the "narrowed limits prescribed for girls and women," and argued that the "race of man needs the inspiration of strong virile womanhood."[3] By the 1940s, sport had become a "central component of African American college life and urban community recreation," which included women as significant players.[4] Historically Black colleges and universities offered several team opportunities for their students as early as the 1920s. In 1948, Henderson was still offering his view that Black girls could be both athletic and feminine when he stated that "colored girls are as a rule, effeminate. They are normal girls."[5] Wilma echoed a similar belief when she wrote, "I loved playing games, and I also loved being a lady after the games. I loved to dress up in pretty outfits just like any other girl."[6] Both comments reflect common thinking of the time period—the misperception that if a female participated in sports she would take on masculine characteristics. A great deal of energy was spent trying to prove that a female could be both feminine and play sport. While this was true for females, both Black and White, Black girls faced tougher codes of behavior based on social class, which connected physicality and working outside of the home with masculinity. On the other hand, Wilma also felt that some of her teammates were lazy and let ideas about womanhood get in the way of playing sports. Wilma also began to express an interest in boys. She didn't like that her girlfriends would choose to not play a sport because a boy might not approve. In her autobiography, Wilma makes the first mention of a boy in her seventh grade year. His name was Robert Eldridge.

As an eighth grader, Wilma was a member of the basketball team and for the second year in a row sat on the bench. She suspected that Coach Gray had only kept her on the team because her older sister was on the team. Coach Gray put Wilma in at the end of a few games when the outcome had already been decided. It was in one of these games that Wilma finally scored her first basket, a one-handed push shot. Coach Gray is credited with giving Wilma her nickname, "Skeeter," which was a slang word for a mosquito. Coach Gray thought that Wilma buzzed around the gym like a mosquito and the name stuck into Wilma's adulthood.

At the end of Wilma's second basketball season, Coach Gray decided to start a new team for the girls at Burt High School, a track team.[7] He asked his basketball players if any of them were interested and Wilma signed up. She thought it would give her something to do since basketball season had ended. The track season lasted from March to May, and the runners wore the basketball uniforms. They did not have any track meets that first season, but had playdays, where everyone received ribbons, and fun was the name of the game. Playdays were common for girls starting in the 1920s, and it involved inviting girls from a number of schools together to form mixed teams to play against each other in a variety of sports. Competition was not emphasized nor encouraged at playdays. After the games, there would often be a time for socializing with the girls from the other schools, sometimes tea and cookies might be shared between the girls. Playdays were designed to promote participation in sports as opposed to competition. In the summer, Wilma played in different sport programs offered by the city recreation department.[8] All of Wilma's sporting experiences at this point in her young life were segregated. Her basketball team played Black teams from other Black high schools. Playdays and other school activities were also segregated.

Wilma was excited for ninth grade. She felt like she had paid her dues in basketball, sitting on the bench for two years and practicing each summer. She was ready to prove to Coach Gray that she was a star player. Yet for the third straight season, Wilma spent the majority of the games on the bench. When she confronted Coach Gray about her lack of playing time, he let her scrimmage against the first string team, but she continued to sit on the bench much to her disappointment. She felt like she was a better shooter, rebounder, and player than some of her teammates who were playing. Wilma was frustrated; for three years, she had been sitting on the bench and had little to show for her practice efforts. By the time basketball season ended and track season started, she was ready to show that she was more than just a bench warmer.

During her freshman year on the track team, Coach Gray arranged for several track meets between Burt High School and other schools from Springfield, Columbia, and Murfreesboro, school teams that Burt High had competed against in basketball. Wilma recalled that the meets were very disorganized and that the focus seemed to be more about having fun rather than competition. During that season, she ran the 50-, 75-, 100-, and 200-yard dashes, along with the relay. She won every race that season, though the major emphasis was still on having fun. Reflecting back on her first years in track, Wilma recognized that she was winning through her natural ability and not from hard work or training. She had no real knowledge related to the technical aspects of running, and Coach Gray was a basketball coach who simply started the team to keep his players busy and in shape. She remembered running in tennis shoes on tracks that had no lanes. Sometimes she didn't even know where the finish line was! She remembered winning 20 races that spring and that she never lost a race. Even though basketball was her first love, she started to recognize that she was very good at running, and she loved the ways that running made her feel. Other people noticed her talent on the track and suggested she focus on the sport that she was winning, instead of the sport where she didn't even get to play. Still, Wilma loved basketball and was confident that with three years under her belt as a team member she would finally become a starter. She had paid her dues and was determined to have Coach Gray recognize her talents on the basketball court.

Entering the tenth grade, Wilma had grown to almost six feet tall and weighed only a little more than 100 pounds. She resolved to become a starter on the basketball team and practiced with a determination that impressed her coach. She and her best friend and classmate, Nancy Bowen, who had also spent the last three years on the bench, had decided to practice and prepare for the season. They wanted to make sure Coach Gray would finally notice their athletic talents and put them in the games. That preseason, Coach Gray was supervising the practices in the gym for the annual "minstrel show" and Wilma and Nancy would convince him to let them practice at the other end of the gym.[9] They would shoot, dribble, and oftentimes play against boys until Coach Gray would kick them all out of the gym. Still, Wilma and Nancy felt that their extra practices were having an impact on Coach Gray. Another teammate, Delma, moved into the Rudolph household because she lived far from the school and it was hard to get home after practice. Wilma and Nancy started to include Delma and another teammate, Ruth Fletcher, in their special practices. All four girls were sophomores, and were playing very well together at preseason practices. The first night of the season, Wilma and her three friends started their first game for Burt High as tenth graders and began to make their mark on the world of Tennessee girls basketball.

At a round-robin tournament held in the Burt High School gymnasium in front of her school mates, Wilma once scored 32 points and, according to her autobiography, did not miss a single shot that day. She wrote, "I was somebody in school after that, for the first time."[10] Her accomplishments in sport boosted her spirits and made her feel better about herself. One thing that she disliked about the basketball season was the ways that Coach Gray would yell at her in front of her teammates. To be singled out in such a negative way was embarrassing to Wilma, and she would often quit the team, only to be back at practice the next day. Besides coaching girls basketball and track, Coach Gray also coached football, and Wilma did not think he made more than $200 each sport season. She remembered him as a dedicated coach, despite his penchant for yelling.

The team ended Wilma's sophomore season with 11 wins and 4 losses, and Burt High School claimed the Middle East Tennessee Conference title, the league for the Black high schools in the area. As a sophomore, she scored 803 points in 25 games, setting a scoring record for girls basketball in Tennessee.[11] Claiming the conference title qualified the team for the Tennessee High School Girls Championships at Pearl High School in Nashville. The championships were also segregated competitions. The team stayed over night at Coach Gray's sister's house in Nashville for the tournament. After winning their first game, with Wilma scoring 28 points and Nancy Bowen scoring 30 points, the team was geared up to win the title. Instead they lost the next game and were eliminated from the championship tournament finishing in third place.[12] It was a disappointing loss for the team, and the girls took it hard. Still, Wilma realized that she was only a sophomore, and they would be better next year.

Once basketball season ended, Wilma focused all of her attention on the new track season. By this time she was dating Robert Eldridge, her seventh grade crush, and would often spend time with him after practice. She sometimes skipped classes to run on the track for extra practice until the principal threatened to call her father to report her truancy. She was eager to continue her victorious ways on the track and knew that she was getting better. That season, the Burt High team was invited to a weekend track meet hosted by Tuskegee Institute, in Tuskegee, Alabama, a historically Black university.[13] The Tuskegee Relays were created in 1936 by the Tuskegee Coach Major Cleveland Abbott. The Tuskegee Relays was the "proving ground" for young Black girls from Southern states. Some of the better athletes were selected to train at Tuskegee's summer program and ultimately offered athletic scholarships to run for Coach Abbott as part of the Tuskegee Institute track team. For 20 years, Tuskegee dominated women's track and won the national Amateur Athletic Union (AAU) champion every year from 1937 to 1956, with the exception of 1952. Though the Tuskegee Relays were only for Black schools and Tuskegee was an all-Black college, AAU championships were integrated competition, making

Tuskegee's dominance all the more significant an accomplishment for the Southern school.

Wilma's Burt High School team was simply excited to compete at Tuskegee, because besides the track meet there was going to be a big dance after the races. The social aspects of the sport setting for girls were still important. Coach Gray drove the team to Alabama in his car, and Wilma's former teacher and Brownie troop leader, Mrs. Allison, accompanied the team as a chaperone. Coach Gray prepared them on the ride down to Tuskegee telling the girls that they would be facing tough competition from other schools that were able to practice year-round because they lived in warmer climates. Once the Burt High School team arrived, they realized that the races would be more challenging than their regular track meets. They were all nervous, including Wilma. It was the first time many of the girls had ever been to a college campus and everything was overwhelming. Wilma recalled that she had been a little cocky before the races, because she was so used to winning every race she ran. This meet turned out a little differently for Wilma—she didn't win a single race! Years later, in remembering the track meet, she wrote "I was totally crushed... It was the first time I had ever tasted defeat in track, and it left me a total wreck... I can't remember ever being so totally crushed by anything."[14] She remembered being so despondent over losing that she skipped the dance and didn't talk the entire ride home. Wilma did not take losing easily.

The girls from Georgia, Alabama, and other Southern states had left a strong impression on Wilma. The losses at Tuskegee were sobering for Wilma and helped her to recognize that she could not win every race simply on her natural ability; she had to practice to become better. She would often pretend to be sick at school so she could go outside and run on the track. Sometimes teachers would allow her to leave class to have extra practice! Wilma won the rest of her races that track season, but always remembered the lessons she learned at Tuskegee. The Tuskegee losses impacted the way she felt about herself and were connected to her self-esteem. This is evident in reading her autobiography when she reveals "Some days I just wanted to go out and die. I just moped around and felt sorry for myself. My confidence was shattered and I was thinking that the only way I could put it all together was to get back the next year and wipe them all out."[15] Despite this depressed feeling and the sting of the Tuskegee losses, Wilma admitted later in her life that her behavior was extreme and that the real value of losing was learning how to pick herself back up and run again. That, she felt, was the important lesson sport could offer, though it took a number of years before she could acknowledge this.

Wilma remembered that during her sophomore basketball season there was a referee that seemed to take a special interest in her. Sometimes the referee would tell Wilma and Coach Gray that she was lazy. His name was Ed Temple, and after games he would suggest drills for her to do to improve her skills. Instead of being upset at the referee for his criticisms, she heeded his advice. One drill he suggested was to jump up to a target on a wall to improve her vertical jump. As she got better, Coach Gray would move the target higher. Temple was also the track coach at Tennessee State College, and years later Wilma realized that Temple was scouting her for his track team. At the end of the season, Coach Temple, the basketball referee, approached Ed and Blanche Rudolph to invite Wilma to attend his summer track program at Tennessee State University in Nashville. He told them that training in his summer program would hopefully lead to Wilma attending Tennessee State University after she finished high school, an idea that pleased her parents. Temple's summer program was modeled after Coach Abbott's summer program at Tuskegee Institute. Only a few years after taking her leg braces off, Wilma Rudolph was already making her mark on the basketball court and the track. Meeting Coach Temple would change Wilma's life forever.

NOTES

1. Burt High School was named for Dr. Robert Tecumseh Burt (1873–1955), a medical doctor. Burt opened the first hospital in Clarksville, Tennessee, in 1916.

2. Susan Cahn, Coming on Strong: Gender and Sexuality in Twentieth-Century Women's Sport (New York: The Free Press, 1994), 117.

3. Cahn, Coming on Strong, 117.

4. Cahn, Coming on Strong, 118.

5. Cahn, Coming on Strong, 133.

6. Wilma Rudolph, with Martin Ralbovsky, Wilma: The Story of Wilma Rudolph (New York: Signet, 1977), 43–44.

7. According to "World Speed Queen," New York Times, 9 September 1960, 20, Coach Ed Temple at Tennessee A & I asked Coach Gray to start a track team to develop one of Gray's forwards for sprinting.

8. Joan Ryan, Contributions of Women: Sports (Minneapolis, MN: Dillon Press, Inc., 1975), 52.

9. A minstrel show is the equivalent of what today is called a talent show.

10. Rudolph, Wilma, 56.

11. Ryan, Contributions of Women, 52. Also see Larry Schwartz, "Her Roman Conquest," http://espn.go.com/sportscentury/features/00016446.html

(accessed December 18, 2005). The record was among Black high schools. Just as competition was separate between White and Black high schools, records were also kept separately.

12. Schwartz, "Her Roman Conquest"; M. B. Roberts, "Rudolph ran and world went wild," http://espn.go.com/sportscentury/features/00016444.html. ESPN.com (accessed December 18, 2005).

13. Historically Black Colleges and Universities (HBCU's) are institutions established primarily for the education of African Americans.

14. Rudolph, *Wilma*, 63–64.

15. Rudolph, *Wilma*, 65.

Chapter 3

MEETING ED TEMPLE AND RUNNING WITH THE TENNESSEE STATE TIGERBELLES

Any coach will tell you if you run across one great athlete in a lifetime, it is a thrill and an honor. To bring a person up through the amateur ranks and see them qualify is the Utopia of all amateurism.[1]

—Ed Temple

Ed Temple first noticed Wilma Rudolph's athletic skills when he refereed her basketball games at Burt High School. He was a sociology professor and women's track coach at Tennessee State College. He drove the Tennessee State track team to meets in his own car and maintained the school track with his own money. He was dedicated to making his team the best athletes they could be.

Born on September 20, 1927, and raised in Harrisburg, Pennsylvania, Edward Stanley Temple was the only child of Christopher and Ruth Temple. Temple was an all-state athlete in track and field, basketball, and football at John Harris High School. For the most part, he was one of only a few African Americans on his sport teams. Unlike Wilma, his high school sport career was always in integrated settings, as was his high school education. In his autobiography, Coach Temple recalls the opposing team's cheerleaders chanting, "Get that nigger!" during a basketball game. Similar incidents occurred in football.[2] Temple attended Tennessee State University after graduating from high school in 1946. Recruited by Pennsylvania State University, Temple turned the school down to attend

Tennessee State after hearing that his high school rival, Leroy Craig, was enrolling at Tennessee State. Once there, both Temple and Craig realized they had been tricked; each had been told that the other was attending Tennessee State, prompting them both to attend the Southern school to continue their rivalry, this time as teammates. Temple received no athletic scholarship and was fortunate to find a campus job to pay his tuition. He had a difficult time adjusting to the color line and the accompanying segregated practices in the South, as he had lived his entire life in an integrated setting.

A Health and Physical Education major, Temple was a sprinter at Tennessee State running the 100-yard dash in 9.7 seconds and the 200-yard dash in 21.5 seconds. In July 1950, Temple married his wife, Charlie, after meeting her in a physiology class. They had two children together, Lloyd Bernard and Edwina. Temple completed his bachelor's degree and remained at Tennessee State to earn his masters degree in Health and Physical Education. While working on his master's degree, Temple accepted the assistant coach position for the women's track and field team and later that year became the head coach. Temple also worked at the campus post office and often employed his runners at the post office to help cover their tuition. Tennessee State President Walter Davis paid Temple $150 a week for both jobs.[3] Instead of offering female athletes scholarships for their athletic ability, they would be offered work positions on campus to cover their school fees. Athletic scholarships were reserved for male athletes only. It wasn't until after the 1964 Olympic Games in Tokyo, where four of his Tigerbelles won six of the seven American medals in track and field and a meeting between Temple and the Tennessee Governor, Buford Ellington, that Tennessee State began to offer athletic scholarships to the female athletes.[4]

When Temple entered the coaching profession, Tuskegee Coach Cleveland Abbott was the big name in coaching women's track. Coach Abbott had a philosophy that was inclusive and worked to "provide a medium whereby Negro girls would be able to exercise athletic talents in this particular activity."[5] Even if his philosophy was not focused on winning, Abbott's Tuskegee track team was undefeated from 1937 to 1942.[6] The success of Abbott's team was inspiring to other historically Black colleges and universities and in 1943, Tennessee State's president, Walter Davis, started a women's track team. The first coach of the women's team at Tennessee State was Jessie Abbott, the daughter of Tuskegee's Cleveland Abbott. She coached for two years before stepping down and returning to her teaching and administrative duties. Tom Harris, a former

football coach, took the position and for four years coached both the
men's and women's track and field teams. It was Harris who had initially
recruited Temple to run for Tennessee State and who he eventually left
the position to in 1953.[7]

In contrast to Cleveland Abbott, Coach Temple opted to limit his
focus and concentrate on achieving victory, preparing his few athletes for
demanding world-class competition. After Cleveland Abbott's death in
1955, Tennessee State surpassed Tuskegee as the dominant women's track
program in the United States—Black or White. Temple started his own
summer track program in 1954 which was established to teach basic track
skills and expose them to Tennessee State campus experience, imitating
the successful summer program that Coach Abbott had run at Tuskegee.
In 1955, Temple started the Tennessee State University Relays, modeled
after Abbott's Tuskegee Relays. Temple credited Abbott with having a
great influence on his coaching.

As a coach, Temple was very demanding of his athletes. Practice ses-
sions were 90 minutes of organized and disciplined training. Techniques
such as the 'Tennessee lean' at the finish line and baton passing for the
relay were practiced over and over. Temple mandated that practice was
year-round with his athletes running cross country in the fall, competing
at indoor meets each winter, and outdoor meets in the spring. He continued to build his summer program to develop high school runners that
would eventually join his college team. Temple believed that a runner
who had attended his summer program would have a much easier time
adjusting to the rigors of competing as a Tigerbelle at the college level.
Nearly 90 percent of the girls who attended the summer camp eventually
enrolled at Tennessee State.

The accounts of how Wilma first was invited to attend Temple's camp
vary, depending on who tells the story. In her autobiography, Wilma
asserts that after seeing her play basketball, Coach Temple recruited her
to attend his summer track program in Nashville. In another account of
Wilma's life, it is suggested that Coach Gray contacted Coach Temple
about inviting his young runner to the college program.[8] It is important
to determine the timetable, because if one is to go along with Wilma's
account, then Wilma was invited after her sophomore year of playing
basketball and her first summer of the track program was 1956, the same
year she qualified and competed in the Olympic Games in Melbourne,
Australia. Such a transition from being a high school athlete to an
Olympian in one summer would have been remarkable. If the other
accounts of her track career at Tennessee State's summer program are
accurate, then Wilma actually attended the summer program after

her freshman year in high school and since she had not played much in basketball, it would have been difficult for Coach Temple to have seen her play, though not impossible. Because accounts do exist that establish Wilma's participation in the 1955 AAU meet in Ponca City, Oklahoma, it is assumed that she was incorrect in her timetable.[9] Even Coach Temple's recollection in his autobiography may be off by a year. He recalls Wilma attending the very first year of the summer program in 1954 and remembered Wilma as a "young, gangling 14-year-old."[10] Coach Temple recalled that Wilma was "an excellent basketball player," but "inexperienced as a runner." She worked with his team during the summer of 1955 and by the next year was on the all-TSU relay at the Olympic Games.[11] She also does not say how the first summer helped her high school track career as she only explains how she changed after running in the Olympics in 1956. One has to assume that attending a college summer track program would have a significant impact on both her running as well as recognizing her aspirations to later attend college.

According to her own accounts, it took a considerable amount of negotiating to convince Wilma's parents to let her go away for the summer at the young age of 15, but Temple was tenacious. He told them about his curfew rules, assured them that Wilma would be supervised by Marian Armstrong-Perkins, the chaperone who stayed in the dorm with the girls, and that all expenses would be covered. Armstrong-Perkins served as Temple's assistant coach at the summer program between 1958 and 1963. Coach Temple felt that Coach Armstrong-Perkins was one of the best female coaches he ever worked with. Not only did she assist Coach Temple for many years, she also helped recruit girls from Georgia to attend Tennessee State.[12] Still, Ed Rudolph felt that his daughter was too young to leave home for the summer, though he finally relented and allowed her to attend. Wilma's mother was more supportive, telling her young daughter, "You're the first one in this house that ever had the chance to go to college. If running's going to do that, I want you to set your mind to be the best! Never give up."[13] Since her daughter had been in leg braces, Mrs. Rudolph had always believed Wilma would one day be able to walk and the opportunity to run with Coach Temple was a great reward for years of hard work, effort, and faith. Wilma was headed to Nashville for the summer.

On the drive to Nashville, Coach Temple and Wilma talked about basketball. Wilma stayed in the dorms with other girls who were attending the summer program. In her autobiography, she states that she roomed with Martha Hudson that first summer, though because her time table is inaccurate, she must have roomed with Hudson her second summer of 1956, which she remembered as her first. Her first summer, actually in 1955, Coach Gray drove her to Nashville every day, an arrangement that helped secure her parents' permission.[14] Martha was also a basketball player in her hometown of Twin City High School in McRae, Georgia. She had competed at the Tuskegee Relays, and 1955 was the first summer that she had been invited to train with Temple and the Tigerbelle summer program. She was very short, only 4 feet 10 inches and Tigerbelle Mae Faggs, who was also very short, nicknamed her "Peewee." Martha, Wilma, and Mae, would later become teammates at Tennessee State.[15]

Temple's equipment manager Pappy Marshall issued the girls a few t-shirts, some Converse basketball shoes, and some shorts. If one is to believe Wilma's account of the fist two weeks of practice, which were the cross country phase, Temple had them running up to 20 miles a day to build up their endurance.[16] The girls were woken up before 6 A.M. and would run six miles, and then they had breakfast. They would rest until around 10:30 A.M. and run another six miles before lunch. They would rest after lunch until 3 P.M. and then run another six miles. This was the daily routine. It might be easier to believe that they ran 20 miles a week, and it seems likely that she could have been exaggerating; for a sprinter, any distance beyond a mile seems like a marathon! The cross country phase helped to build Wilma's stamina. The girls would relax and rest on the weekends, going to church, playing cards, and socializing with visitors. Wilma's brothers and sisters, and her boyfriend, Robert, visited frequently on weekends throughout the summer.

Eventually the girls were given track shoes and focused on shorter distances. Temple taught the girls proper running techniques. Wilma remembered learning small, but important things, such as learning to keep her fists loose, how to stay relaxed, and breathing patterns. She also worked on starts, which had always given her trouble. Wilma had poor reflexes coming out of the starting blocks, and it took her some time to get acceleration in her races. In high school races, she had never used starting blocks, but she knew that a better start would mean a better finish. She practiced her starts all summer.

Temple emphasized the team atmosphere, and there was a competitive spirit that pervaded the group of talented runners. On the track they would compete against each other, and off the track they remained friendly. Temple would split the girls into the Blue and White squads, and students on campus would show up to watch the two squads compete. Temple would conduct the intersquad competition like a real track meet and times were recorded and team scores tallied. Wilma did not win every race, but she often beat the college runners and soon realized that she was getting better even if she didn't win every race. The first summer with the Tigerbelles was a tremendous learning experience for Wilma, but apparently the power of the lessons faded when she wrote about it in her autobiography, as she failed to mention it!

That first summer, the National Amateur Athletic Union outdoor championships were hosted in Ponca City, Oklahoma. Led by Mae Faggs, the Tigerbelle team won their first AAU title with 87.5 points, and their closest competition, the Chicago Comets finished with 59 points.[17] After the AAU victory, the Tigerbelles' success received national recognition. Coach Temple claimed that the first AAU title was a great thrill for him, but also a disappointment. He remembered, "I was on cloud nine because I knew it was the first time a black school had ever won a national championship. But the people at Tennessee State didn't appreciate it. They were still thinking of us as a black team who won the black championship. They didn't know the significance of being a national champion. Really, we just advanced too fast for the school at the time. There is no doubt about it. We were way ahead of them."[18] *Sports Illustrated* proclaimed that TSU was "fast becoming the Notre Dame of women's track and field," while the *New York Times* wrote "The cathedral of women's track in this country is Tennessee A&I and Temple is its high priest."[19]

Wilma's autobiography mentions nothing about the Ponca City debut of the Tigerbelles or her own initial AAU competition. Perhaps this is because she did not win one race, finishing 4th in the 75-yard dash behind roommate Martha Hudson and teammate Lucinda Williams, and finishing 2nd in the 100-yard dash. She competed in the girls' junior division, while the older Tigerbelles competed in the senior division. Wilma also fails to mention the AAU track meets as the first integrated competitions she participated in. Previously, every playday, high school track meet, and high school basketball game had been against other Black girls. AAU track meets were integrated and had Black and White girls running against each other and with each other on the same team. It seems likely that Wilma did not include the Ponca City experience, as well as her first summer at Tennessee State, in her own autobiography because it was not part of the narrative she later established that was about her success in track, rather than her failures. But in many ways, that summer of 1955 fits completely into the narrative that Wilma crafted over the years—that first summer of not being the best must have been very motivating to the young Wilma, it must have influenced her as she returned to Burt High School, and it most certainly must have helped shape her ideas about winning and losing and impacted how she felt about herself. It is unfortunate that she chose not to recall such instances, as they certainly would have been very revealing about her development as a young runner. However, Wilma was able to recall her first summer full of great successes—the summer of 1956—Tigerbelles, AAU titles, and Olympic dreams. For a girl who had struggled to walk as a child, it was amazing that her legacy was being built on running.

Wilma returned to Coach Temple's summer program at Tennessee State in the summer of 1956. Coach Temple decided to put Wilma with three other high school girls, Martha Hudson, Willye White, and Annette Anderson to form a junior relay team. The high school foursome was routinely beat by the older college relay competitors, but the margin of victory kept getting smaller and smaller. The younger girls would tease the older girls that they would eventually beat them. Reflecting back on her relay team's performances against the older girls, Wilma explained that one of the reasons they did not beat the older relay was out of respect for the college girls and the desire to be liked by the older group. Whether this was the reality is hard to determine, but at points in her running career, Coach Temple certainly encouraged Wilma to not ease up at the end of a race to allow others to win. Coach Temple was preparing the junior relay team for the 1956 National AAU championship in Philadelphia at the end of the summer. In the weeks preceding the AAU meet, the relay practiced baton handoffs over and over. At different points in the summer, Wilma ran every leg of the relay except the first leg, which would have required her to start out of the blocks. She was not good at using the starting blocks. Eventually, Wilma settled into the anchor role.

The team drove to Philadelphia in a caravan of station wagons and according to Wilma, it was the first time she had stayed in such a big city.[20] The track meet was held at Franklin Field, where the Penn Relays are hosted every spring on the University of Pennsylvania campus. Wilma was entered in the 75-yard, 100-yard, and the 440-yard relay in the girls' junior division, meaning that she would be competing against other high school girls. Qualifying heats started early in the morning and there were two trials in each race to whittle the 50 to 60 entrants down to a final 8. She won every race she entered that day, including the relay, and Tennessee State, with only five girls on the junior team, won the National AAU meet in the junior division. Press coverage of track and field during that time was very scarce, and Wilma remembered that "none of us even thought about looking in the sports pages the next day for writeups because we knew automatically that nobody would bother to write us up. It was like, oh, well, girls' track, that's not really a sports event."[21] The team stayed over night in Philadelphia to watch the senior Tigerbelle team compete and win the AAU title the next day.

Besides not receiving much press attention, Wilma remembered that Coach Temple was not big on celebrations, even after winning two National AAU titles! He was quiet throughout track meets and would encourage the girls to rest in between their races. According to Wilma, he never congratulated the girls for their performances; it wasn't his style. Temple explained his philosophy as one that "has always been to walk soft and carry a heavy stick. You don't have to whoop and holler and say what you're going to do. You just got to get the job done."[22] Wilma recalled her coach saying something to her like "You're coming along real well, Wilma, you've got a lot of potential," but that was the extent of his praise. Wilma was extremely pleased with her AAU performance and was feeling confident about her running.[23]

One other exciting event that occurred to Wilma at the AAU meet in Philadelphia was the opportunity to meet Jackie Robinson, the Brooklyn Dodger baseball player who had re-integrated major league baseball a decade earlier, and his teammate, pitcher Don Newcombe, who was also African American. The three posed for photos together. Though Wilma rarely acknowledged the accomplishments of other African American athletes in her autobiography, she does admit to admiring Robinson and the thrill she felt meeting the famous ballplayer.[24] Robinson's breaking of the color barrier in major league baseball, the nation's hallowed pastime, was a significant social event in American history, preceding the integration of both the military and educational institutions. To much of Black America, as well as White America, the boundary breaking Robinson represented the promises of integration and a shift in race relations.[25] It also confirmed for many Americans the meritocracy of the sporting landscape—the best players emerged due to their talent and performances, not because of the color of their skin or family heritage.

Meeting Jackie Robinson was quite a memory for Wilma. Wilma was initially shy and somewhat embarrassed about her Southern accent, but ended up having a great conversation with the famous ballplayer and having her picture taken with him. She remembered Robinson telling her that he liked her running, and he thought she had a lot of potential. Robinson had run track at UCLA, along with playing football and baseball. They talked about what grade she was in at school, living in Tennessee, and how long she had been running. Robinson was surprised that Wilma was as young as she was and replied "You are a fascinating runner and don't let anything, or anybody, keep you from running. Keep running." The encounter was overwhelming for young Wilma, but she was excited to have met Robinson and felt that for the first time in her life she had a Black person to look up to as a real hero.[26]

After the AAU meet in Philadelphia, Coach Temple told Wilma that she might have a chance to run in the Olympic Games and should "give it a try."[27] She recalls that as a teenager she really had no concept of what the Olympics were; she had no idea that athletes from around the world competed against each other. She had never even heard of Melbourne, Australia, which was where the 1956 Olympics were being held later that year. The Olympic Trials, a track meet to determine the Olympic team, were two weeks after the Philadelphia meet, and Coach Temple assured her that the training she had done all summer would be preparation enough for the Trials, which would be held in Washington, D.C.[28]

Coach Temple drove Wilma and his college team to the Trials. On the trip with Wilma were Margaret Mathews, Isabelle Daniels, Willye White, Lucinda Williams, and Mae Faggs. Wilma identified Mae Faggs as the senior girl on the team and the person most responsible for helping her to become a competitive runner (after Coach Temple of course). Mae had already competed in the Olympic Games and was like a second coach to Wilma and the other runners. She was very small, standing at only 5 feet 2 inches, prompting teammates to call her "Little Mae." Mae started running with the Police Athletic League team run by officer John Brennan in Bayshore, New York, and when she was only 14 years old entered the 1948 Olympic Trials hosted in Providence, Rhode Island. She finished third in the 200-meter race behind Tennessee State Tigerbelle Audrey Patterson and Nell Jackson, the captain of the Tuskegee team, qualifying Mae as the youngest member of the U.S. Olympic team. At the 1948 Olympics, which were held in London, England, Mae finished third in her heat behind the eventual Olympic gold medalist Fanny Blankers-Koen and was eliminated from the competition. Teammate Alice Coachman told Mae, "You're just beginning. Young as you are, you can be in two or three Olympic Games."[29] In 1949, Mae ran in her first AAU national indoor meet. At the 1952 Olympic Trials in Buffalo, New York, Mae finished first in the 100-meter race, second in the 200-meter race, and became the only member from the 1948 U.S. Olympic team to win a spot on the 1952 team for the Olympic Games in Helsinki, Finland. The expectations for the United States were low, because the Soviet Union dominated women's track and field. In fact, the 1952 Olympic Games were the first Olympic competition for the Soviet Union, and they made the most of their Olympic debut. The Soviet athletes came in second in the total medal count behind the United States.[30] The American team scored only 1 point in individual events, when Mae finished 6th in the

100-meter race. The highlight was the American 4x100-meter relay team of Faggs, Barbara Jones, Janet Moreau (who was White), and Catherine Hardy, winning a gold medal and setting a new world record in 45.9 seconds.

After the 1952 Olympics, Mae attended Tennessee State on a work scholarship. However, the Tennessee State track team was not very good, with only Mae and Cynthia Thompson making up the small Tigerbelle team. Coach Temple recalled that when Mae enrolled at Tennessee State, "she had the experience to be cocky" based on her being on the 1948 and 1952 Olympic teams and claimed that his new runner knew more about track than he did! He felt that Tennessee State was fortunate to have a runner of Mae's caliber and experience on the Tigerbelle team.[31] Because there was no money to pay for the team to travel to track meets, Mae was unable to defend her 200-meter race AAU title that she had held since 1949. In fact, the Tigerbelle team competed in just one track meet that year, the Tuskegee Relays. As more students came out for the team, including Lucinda Williams and Isabelle Daniels, the Tigerbelles became more competitive. The real turning point for the team was winning their first AAU outdoor national championship title in Ponca City, Oklahoma, in 1955, led by Mae Faggs.[32] Only one year later, Mae and Wilma were competing at the 1956 Olympic Trials as teammates.

Wilma looked up to Mae as an experienced runner and remembered Mae talking to her before the Trials, encouraging her to start thinking about herself as an individual rather than being focused on fitting in with the group. This was a valuable, but difficult lesson for a teenage girl competing against college runners. Wilma was so concerned with being liked and accepted by her older teammates, that she sometimes did not race as hard as she could, often losing to her teammates when it seemed like she could have won. Mae told Wilma, "You really have the ability to perform as an individual."[33] Mae was giving Wilma permission to start running her best and not hold back for fear that her teammates would dislike her if she beat them. These lessons would be invaluable for Wilma. At the Olympic Trials she would be competing against her summer teammates and to qualify for the Olympics would require her to beat her teammates. Coach Temple had also noticed Wilma's tendency to hold back in certain races and specifically put her on the relay team to work on this problem. She admitted to easing up to let the older girls win, even in a relay. She felt that as a high school runner she should not show up the college runners. The talk from Mae Faggs helped her to focus on her own performance in each race and to be more concerned with her own individual performances.

The team relaxed for a few days prior to the Olympic Trials. Wilma remembers that about 50 to 60 girls were there for the track meet. Once the meet started, Wilma was anxious and was unable to eat before her races. She was entered in the 200-meter race and the 4x100-meter relay. Before her races, Mae saw how nervous her young teammate was and told Wilma to stick with her in the 200-meter race. Mae thought that if Wilma could stay with her throughout the race, she would make the team. They finished in a dead heat with the same time and after the race, Mae went up to Wilma and said "I told you to stick with me, I didn't tell you to beat me. You know, as soon as this thing is over, I'm going to retire. I think you've made it, you're ready to replace me right now. You really beat me in that race. What took you so long to get there? We've all known you had it in you, but we all wondered when it would come out. Today it did."[34] Later, Mae reminded her that when Wilma ran her best and ran to win, she really helped the team. As a result of her finish in the 200-meter race, Wilma qualified for the 1956 Olympic Games and was headed to Melbourne, Australia. Both Mae and Wilma were selected for the relay team, along with Tigerbelle teammates Margaret Mathews and Isabelle Daniels. Mae became the only athlete from the 1952 team to win a spot on the 1956 team, her third Olympic team in a row.

Returning from the Trials, a Nashville newspaper wrote an article about Wilma, which excited her because she finally was in the newspaper. Clarksville was also excited to send one of their own citizens off to the Olympics, and some local people donated clothes and luggage for Wilma to head to Australia in style. Her family did not have the money to give to her and she has "never forgotten those people to this day...I love them dearly for the help they gave me when I most needed it."[35] The town had a send-off for Wilma, and she was on her way to Australia as the youngest member of the women's track and field team, just as her friend and teammate Mae Faggs had been in 1948.

NOTES

1. Dwight Lewis and Susan Thomas, *A Will to Win* (Mt. Juliet, TN: Cumberland Press, 1983), 125. Temple was referring to his experience coaching Wilma Rudolph.

2. Ed Temple, with B'Lou Carter, *Only the Pure in Heart Survive* (Nashville, TN: Broadman Press, 1980), 17–18.

3. Lewis and Thomas, *A Will to Win*, 115.

4. Temple, *Only the Pure in Heart*, 31.

5. Marianna W. Davis (ed.), *Contributions of Black Women to America: Volume I* (Columbia, SC: Kenday Press, Inc., 1982), 525.

6. A. S. "Doc" Young, *Negro Firsts in Sports* (Chicago: Johnson Publishing Company Inc., 1963), 196.

7. Lewis and Thomas, *A Will to Win*, 108.

8. Joan Ryan's account has Coach Temple noticing Wilma in a tournament in Nashville and telling the young runner, "You're a natural runner. I'd like to help coach you," 54; see Joan Ryan, *Contributions of Women: Sports* (Minneapolis: Dillon Press, 1975). Ryan's account also credits Coach Gray with driving Wilma to Tennessee State every day in the summer so she could be coached by Coach Temple. Janet Woolum's account in *Outstanding Women Athletes: Who They Are and How They Influenced Sports in America* (Phoenix, AZ: Oryx Press, 1992), 48, also has Wilma attending the summer camp in 1955 and having Coach Gray drive her daily.

9. One account is found in Bobby Lovett, "Leaders of Afro-American Nashville: Wilma Rudolph and the TSU Tigerbelles," 1997 Nashville Conference on Afro-American Culture and History, located in Sacramento State University archives. It states that Wilma was invited in the summer of 1955 at the age of 14. She would have turned 15 the summer of 1955.

10. Temple, *Only the Pure in Heart*, 21.

11. Temple, *Only the Pure in Heart*, 63.

12. Temple, *Only the Pure in Heart*, 34.

13. Alex Haley, "The Girl Who wouldn't Give Up," *Reader's Digest* 78 (May 1961): 144.

14. Chapter 3, note 7 clarifies some of the discrepancies in the accounts of Wilma's first summer with the Tigerbelles.

15. Michael D. Davis, *Black American Women in Olympic Track and Field* (Jefferson, NC: McFarland & Company, Inc., 1992), 73–75.

16. The Tigerbelle training schedule is included in Coach Temple's book; see *Only the Pure in Heart*, 165–72.

17. Lewis and Thomas, *A Will to Win*, 124.

18. Lewis and Thomas, *A Will to Win*, 119.

19. Mary Snow, "Can the Soviet Girls Be Stopped?" *Sports Illustrated*, August 27, 1956, 10–11; Davis, *Black American Women*, 80.

20. Wilma Rudolph, with Martin Ralbovsky, *Wilma: The Story of Wilma Rudolph* (New York: Signet, 1977), 75.

21. Rudolph, *Wilma*, 76–77. According to Wayne Wilson, "Wilma Rudolph: The Making of an Olympic Icon," in *Sport and the Racial Mountain: A Biographical History of the African American Athlete*, ed. David K. Wiggins (Fayetteville: University of Arkansas Press, forthcoming), Wilma also finished second in the 200-meter and was on the winning Tennessee State relay team in the senior division.

22. Lewis and Thomas, *A Will to Win*, 116.

23. Rudolph, *Wilma*, 78.

24. In her autobiography, Wilma mentions three African American athletes that were significant; Jackie Robinson, Olympian high jumper Alice Coachman, and Olympian Mildred McDaniel. She mentions the two women in her final chapter on page 167, though she misidentifies Alice Coachman as a sprinter and the first African American woman to compete in the Olympic Games. Coachman was a high jumper and the first African American to win a gold medal at the Olympic Games. Wilma confuses McDaniel with Coachman stating that McDaniel was the first African American to win a gold medal at the 1956 Olympic Games.

25. For articles, autobiographies and biographies about Jackie Robinson, see Ronald A. Smith, "The Paul Robeson-Jackie Robinson Saga and a Political Collision," *Journal of Sport History* 6 (Summer 1970): 5–27; Jules Tygiel, *Baseball's Great Experiment: Jackie Robinson and His Legacy* (New York: Oxford University Press, 1983); Harvey Frommer, *Rickey and Robinson: The Men Who Broke Baseball's Color Barrier* (New York: MacMillan Publishing Co., 1982); Jackie Robinson, *I Never Had It Made* (New York: G.P. Putnam's Sons, 1971).

26. Rudolph, *Wilma*, 79.

27. Rudolph, *Wilma*, 80.

28. In Wilma's autobiography she remembers incorrectly that the Trials were held in Seattle, Washington, but they were actually held in Washington, D.C., which would not have been such a long drive. It is unclear why she remembers it as Seattle, and even discusses the cold Seattle weather. She also remembered the trip as being first-class; the best motels and restaurants. See Rudolph, *Wilma*, 80–83.

29. Davis, *Black American Women*, 52.

30. The United States tallied a total of 76 medals, including 40 gold, while the Soviets collected 22 gold and a total of 71 medals.

31. Lewis and Thomas, *A Will to Win*, 120.

32. For more on Mae Faggs, see Davis, *Black American Women*, 50–62.

33. Rudolph, *Wilma*, 81.

34. Rudolph, *Wilma*, 84.

35. Rudolph, *Wilma*, 85.

Chapter 4

RUNNING AT THE 1956 OLYMPIC GAMES

The Tennessee State Tigerbelles continued their dominance in women's track and field winning their second straight AAU title in 1956. That same summer, six Tigerbelles tried out for the U.S. women's team to compete at the Melbourne Olympics. All six Tigerbelles made the team. African American women were beginning to dominate American track and field, and the 1956 team was a reflection of this trend.[1]

The success of African American women in track and field competitions was critical to the success of the United States in international competitions. The past inability of American women to fare well in international competition had been of little concern to American sport officials. However, historian Susan Cahn noted that "with the Soviet Union's first Olympic appearance in 1952, these failings posed an acute problem for U.S. politicians, sports leaders, and a patriotic public. The U.S. men's team ranked even with or above Soviet men, but the Soviet women so overpowered their American counterparts that the United States was in danger of losing the unofficial highly publicized competition for Olympic gold."[2] Cold War politics, which pitted the United States versus the Soviet Union, were being played out on athletic fields, and the United States desperately sought to exert their political, cultural, and athletic superiority over their communist counterparts. Clearly, for reasons having more to do with winning and international prominence on the political front and little to do with sensitivities to racial or gender equality, African American women stepped into an important role in American athletics.

In assessing the Cold War sporting rivalry between the United States and the Soviet Union, Cahn asserts that "sport became a part of a Cold

War international contest in which the United States and USSR vied not only for athletic laurels but to prove the superiority of capitalism or communism. Under pressure to triumph over Soviet "slave athletics," the national sports establishment focused unprecedented attention on Black and female athletes. American sport officials paid homage to Black competitors, sheepishly admitting, 'If it weren't for the sensational performances of the great Negro athletes we wouldn't even be in a secondary position in world athletics today.'" Cahn goes on to note the reliance of the American government on "African American talent to disprove Soviet charges of pervasive racial discrimination in U.S. society." Claiming that the prominence of Black athletes in the United States refuted "Communist ideas about the status of our colored citizens," politicians and sports officials championed Black athletic success and the desegregation of major league sports as "an answer to communism."[3] The United States went so far as to distribute pamphlets, books, and films around the world to help explain American politics and race relations.[4]

With the Soviet Union's introduction into Olympic competition in 1952, the communist nation sought to establish their political superiority with their dominance on the athletic playing fields in all of the Olympic sports. The Soviets believed that sporting victories were reflective of the success of their political system, and as such, every victory mattered, including those by their female athletes. This meant that in many ways Soviet women did not face the same gender barriers as their American counterparts when in came to sport participation. Women's track and field during the 1950s was dominated by the Soviet Union, with the American women only beginning to challenge their athletic superiority. The International Olympic Committee had established minimum standards for women's track and field events, though no such standards existed for men. In 9 Olympic track and field events for women, only 10 women could be allowed onto the team, prompting one writer to ask, "How capable of slowing down the Russian steam roller are the rest of the women of the world?"[5] Many supporters of women's track and field were upset about the inequities between the men's and women's participation and believed it "smacks of the Russian attitude of 'Don't compete unless you can win.'"[6] The American women that were capable of competing against and even beating the Russians in the second half of the 1950s included many African American females, such as Barbara Jones, a sprinter from Chicago, and Mae Faggs and Isabelle Daniels from Tennessee Agricultural and Industrial State University, also nicknamed Tennessee State, in Nashville. Mary Snow, of *Sports Illustrated*, noted that if "given one-tenth the support the Russians give their women and still adhering to the American way, our girls could match the Russians next time."[7] When Snow states that the United States would adhere to the American way, she was reinforcing ideas about the Soviet way of supporting their athletes, as well as reminding readers that Americans were true amateurs in sport, something more pure than their Soviet opponents.

One theme that resonated within the media coverage of African American women in sport was the discussion of womanhood. Prior to the 1948 Olympic Games, newspaper writer Fay Young of the *Chicago Defender* predicted in a bold headline, "Negro Women Will Dominate 1948 U.S. Olympic Track Team." Young subtitled his commentary, "Negro Womanhood on Parade," and suggested "that the black public viewed athletics as a terrain of achievement with import beyond the immediate athletic realm."[8] The dialogue concerning the femininity of Black female tracksters was of major importance because of their prominence on the Olympic team and their dominance in AAU competition. There was still concern related to ensuring the femininity of female athletes, especially African American women who were already viewed differently in terms of womanhood due to their skin color and their long history of working outside the home. In the 1950s, African American women made up more than two-thirds of the American track and field team at international track meets, including the Pan American Games and the Olympic Games. While their success on the track was applauded, it simultaneously reinforced the masculine image much of America had of two groups: Black women and female track athletes. "Athletic successes which could, in one context, affirm the dignity and capabilities of African American womanhood, could also appear to confirm derogatory images of both black and athletic women."[9] Track and field officials struggled with how to change the image of American women competing in track and field. But without the talents of African American women in the sport and on the American team, American track and field would languish behind the competition. American sport, and consequently American politics, needed African American women to be competitive with the Soviet Union. The dialogue continued and efforts from within the Black community worked to cultivate a feminine image of African American female track athletes.

The first two African American women to make an Olympic team in any sport were Tidye Pickett and Louise Stokes, who qualified for the 1932 Olympic team in track and field. Louise Stokes was raised in Malten, Massachusetts, and was a member of the Onteora Club track team. She had tied the world record in the standing broad jump, with a leap of 8 feet and 5 3/4 inches. At the 1932 Olympic Trials, Stokes tied for 4th place with Mary Carew in the 100-meter race.[10] Tidye Pickett finished in 6th place in the same race. Pickett was only 17 years old and a student at Englewood High School in Chicago.[11] Both qualified for the American team as part of the 4x100-meter relay, Pickett as an alternate.

On the train trip to Los Angeles, where the Olympic Games were being held, the team stopped in Denver where they stayed in a hotel. Pickett and Stokes were not allowed in the hotel's dining room because they were Black. Both Pickett and Stokes were upset that the United States Olympic Committee allowed them to be treated like second class citizens. Pickett also had a run in with Babe Didrikson, a teammate on the women's track and field squad, when Didrikson threw ice water on her as she lay in her train berth. Though Didrikson explained her behavior as a prank, she made no secret of her dislike for the African Americans on her team. Despite Pickett and Stokes training for the relay, both were removed from the relay team prior to the competition to allow two of their White teammates to run instead.[12] Rus Cowan, writing about the relay slight in the *Chicago Defender*, stated "Lily-whiteism, a thing more pronounced than anything else around here on the eve of the Olympic Games, threatened to oust Tidye Pickett and Louise Stokes from participation and put in their stead two girls who did not qualify."[13] Four years later, Pickett qualified for the 1936 U.S. Olympic team for the Olympic Games held in Berlin, Germany. She competed in the hurdles, but was disqualified in the finals after hitting a hurdle.[14] Stokes did not qualify for the 1936 Games, getting beat by Helen Stephens at the Trials, but she was still selected to travel with the team to room with Pickett. This was a common practice to room Black athletes with other Black athletes. Despite fielding an integrated team, accommodations would have women of the same racial group room together. Pickett went on to have a career in professional bowling.[15] Despite not winning medals at the 1932 or 1936 Olympic Games, both Pickett and Stokes laid a foundation for future African American women to compete at the Olympic Games.[16] When Wilma Rudolph entered the 1956 Olympic Games, she was carrying on the legacy of the two pioneers, Stokes and Pickett.

For two weeks prior to the Olympic Games, the American team trained in Los Angeles. The flight to Los Angeles was the first time Wilma had ever flown in an airplane and when the stewardess asked what she would like to eat, she replied nothing, because she did not want to pay for the food. Luckily, her teammate Mae Faggs was there to let her know that she could order food and not have to pay for it. Mae was also holding onto Wilma's passport for safe keeping. Coach Temple had taken care of the passport arrangements, but wanted the document kept safe with Mae. The long flight to Los Angeles helped Wilma prepare for the even longer trip that lay ahead to Australia. In Los Angeles, the team trained every day at the University of Southern California. Wilma remembered that Los Angeles was very smoggy. Coach Temple was not selected as the coach of the team and did not accompany the team to Australia, but he did try to prepare them for the competition that lay ahead. He had written workouts for each of his Tigerbelle runners during their two-week training camp leading up to the Olympic Games.

The 1956 Olympic U.S. women's track and field team was coached by Nell Jackson, a former athlete and new coach at Tuskegee Institute. Jackson had competed in the 200-meter race and 4x100-meter relay at the 1948 Olympic Games in London, England. The next year, she set the world record in the 200 meters in 24.2 seconds. Coach Jackson was the first African American woman to coach an Olympic track and field team. In 1948, Edwin B. Henderson commented on "the fact that white women held only two of the eleven slots on the 1948 U.S. national track team," saying "American (White) women have been so thoroughly licked over so many years by the Booker T. Washington Girls that they have almost given up track and field competition."[17] The sporting achievements of African American women in track and field "served as a broader symbol of pride and achievement for black communities."[18] At the same time the Black community could recognize these sporting achievements as "measures of black cultural achievement," the athletes were virtually ignored by the White media and athletic establishment.[19]

One of Nell Jackson's Olympic teammates from that 1948 U.S. team, Alice Coachman, a high jumper, was the first African American female athlete to win an Olympic gold medal. Coachman had attended Tuskegee Institute and ran track for the famous Coach Cleveland Abbott in the early 1940s. Because of World War II, the Olympics were cancelled in 1940 and 1944, dashing any Olympic opportunities the Tuskegee track women hoped for. Coachman was one of Tuskegee's star athletes. She was the national outdoor high jump champion from 1939 to 1948 and outdoor 50-meter race champion from 1943 to 1947. In 1946, Coachman was the only African American female selected to the U.S. team for a dual meet with Canada. She won the 100-meter race, the high jump, and anchored the 4x100-meter relay team. At the 1948 Olympic Trials in Providence, Rhode Island, Coachman qualified for the American team in the high jump. Ten African American women made the team and four of those were from Tuskegee; Coachman, Jackson, Theresa Manuel, and Mabel Walker.

After Coachman won the high jump, she returned to the United States and was personally congratulated by President Harry Truman. Alice Coachman Day was set up in Albany, Georgia, and there was a motorcade all the way from Atlanta. Writing in the *Atlanta Daily World*, columnist Marion E. Jackson wrote, "It was not a homecoming for a Negro Olympic star, but a champion of champions. As I watched the faces of thousands of Georgians from all over the state it was interesting to note, that all of their prejudices, preferences, passions and hates were momentarily swept from their countenances as if a heavy rainstorm had drenched a mountainous street.…Reality returned and I knew that Georgia would not make Alice's welcome a wholehearted one.…He [Mayor James W. Smith] never shook her hand nor did he look at her. Alice never got a chance to speak."[20] Mae Faggs had also been a teammate of Jackson and Coachman when she made the team as the youngest member on the 1948 U.S. Olympic team. The African American women on the 1956 team hoped to continue the success of Coachman and return with their own gold medals.

Seventeen American women were named to the 1956 Olympic Track and Field team, with 9 of the 17 women being African American. *Sports Illustrated* had a two page layout of headshots of the women's team, a rare opportunity for sport fans to read about women, but also to see the faces that represented their country. The pictures included in the magazine were the only reference to the color of the runners.[21]

During the two-week training camp, Wilma trained and for the first time really learned about the Olympic Games. Because Mae had been to the Olympics twice, she told Wilma the basic things she would need to know, such as the meaning of the five Olympic rings. Mae explained that the five Olympic rings represented the "five continents linked together in friendly competition."[22] Mae told her that she would get to meet athletes from all over the world and that these friendships would be more meaningful than any medals she might win. Mae really exhibited the Olympic spirit and tried to teach her teammates about it before their trip to Australia. For two weeks, Mae and Wilma trained with their teammates on the relay, Margaret Mathews and Isabelle Daniels, perfecting their handoffs. Margaret, like Wilma, was from a poor family and had grown up in Atlanta. Margaret attended Bethune Cookman College out of high school but didn't like it and decided to attend Tennessee State on a scholarship which covered room, board, and tuition. She had been coached by Marion Armstrong-Perkins (Morgan) at David T. Howard High School.

Coach Armstrong-Perkins had coached other Olympians: Mary McNabb in 1952 and Mildred McDaniel in 1956. At the 1956 Trials, Margaret had set a new American record in the long jump jumping 19 feet and 9 1/2 inches.[23] Her fellow Atlanta native who was also coached by Marion Armstrong-Perkins was high jumper Mildred McDaniel, who like Wilma, played basketball before becoming a high jumper. Mildred attended Tuskegee Institute.

Wilma's other Olympic relay teammate Isabelle "Tweety" Daniels began attending Tennessee State in 1954. Isabelle was a Georgia farm girl and the youngest of nine children. Coach Temple first noticed Isabelle when she won her first race at the Tuskegee Relays running barefoot. Three of Isabelle's siblings had already attended Florida A&M, so going to Tennessee State broke a Daniels' family tradition. At the 1954 outdoor AAU meet in Harrisburg, Pennsylvania, Isabelle was on the winning 4x200-meter relay team with Mae Faggs, Lucinda Williams, and Cynthia Thompson. She was a member of the winning 4x100-meter relay at Ponca City in 1955 with Williams, Faggs, and Martha Hudson and also represented the United States at the Pan-American Games in Mexico City in 1955, where she finished 2nd in the 60-yard race. She had won the AAU indoor championship title in the 50-yard race in 1956 and would retain this title in 1957, 1958, and 1959, setting the world record in the 50-yard race in 1957. Isabelle qualified for the 1956 Games in the 100-meter race and the 4x100-meter relay.[24]

Another Tigerbelle on the 1956 Olympic team was long jumper Willye White, who had been raised by her maternal grandparents in Greenwood, Mississippi. She had earned a spot on the varsity track team at age 10 and began attending the summer running program at Tennessee State in 1956 upon the recommendation of her high school coach. Willye competed in her first national track meet at the 1956 AAU meet in Philadelphia and finished 2nd in the long jump, which qualified her for the Olympic Trials in Washington, D.C.[25]

After two long weeks of training in Los Angeles, the team left for Australia and were assigned to travel with the men's track team. The first stop on the way to Australia was Hawaii. As the athletes got off the plane, they were greeted with dancing girls and flowers. Wilma thought she was in a tropical fantasy world until that night when she and some teammates went shopping. As Wilma described the situation, she and two African American teammates were shopping and as they walked down the street they saw a White woman pick up her dog and cross the street instead of walking by the group. From across the street, the White woman said, "What are you natives doing out in the street?" stunning Wilma and her friends.[26] It didn't matter that they were representing America at the Olympics, to the woman on the street, they were "natives." Fortunately, the team's next stop was the Fiji Islands, which would be a much different experience.

The Fiji Islands were inhabited by "totally black people."[27] Wilma remembers that everyone—police, taxi drivers, airport workers—were all Black. Even though the people were all Black, they did not speak English, which intrigued Wilma. It was on this trip that Wilma began to realize that the world was bigger than Clarksville, bigger than Tennessee, and bigger than the United States. After the stops in Hawaii and the Fiji Islands, the Olympic team was headed on the last leg of the long flight to Melbourne and the Olympic Games.

Once in Australia, the team stayed in the Olympic Village with athletes from all over the world. Athletes from other countries were fascinated with the American athletes and would tell them how much they wanted to visit America. Other athletes asked Wilma for her autograph, and eventually she and her teammates would stand outside the gate to the Olympic Village and sign autographs for whoever wanted them. It was their goodwill gesture, and they were getting into the spirit of the Olympic Games and international camaraderie of Olympic athletes.

The women had separate quarters in the Olympic Village. The athletes had a 9 P.M. curfew and were not allowed to have men in their rooms, and Wilma compared the curfew rules with similar ones that Coach Temple had for his summer program. Wilma didn't think many girls were even interested in men; at that point the only thing they cared about was running in the Olympics. The team had a week to train and get acclimated to the Australian climate. The Olympic Games were held from November 22 to December 9, which fit into the Australian summer, but meant that Wilma missed a great deal of school. Wilma practiced with the relay team and they worked on handoffs every day. Their timing was off and Wilma suspected that part of their lack of focus was a "psychological letdown of not having Coach Temple there."[28]

The opening ceremonies were very exciting and after the parade Wilma met one of her competitors, and hometown favorite, Australian Betty Cuthbert. Wilma and Betty talked about running and track shoes, and Betty showed the American team a pair of track shoes made with kangaroo leather that were light and considered a very fast shoe. Betty told the American women that they could buy a pair in Australia for $20, but Wilma did not have the money and turned down Mae's offer to loan her the money.

Wilma's first race was the trials for the 200-meter race. She finished third and qualified for the next round. In the next round, she finished third again, but only the top two advanced and Wilma was eliminated and did not make it to the finals in the 200-meter race.[29] Feeling like a failure, she was very disappointed in her performance and, despite all efforts to lift her spirits, was miserable about her poor showing. She tried to convince herself that she still had a chance to redeem herself in the relay. She watched from the stands as Australian sprinter Betty Cuthbert won the 100-, 200-, and 400-meter races for three gold medals. Seeing Cuthbert on the stand three times motivated Wilma to do the same and she committed herself to making the Olympic Games in 1960 and to winning a gold medal. Wilma's only shot at a medal was in the 4x100-meter relay and her three teammates were Mae Faggs leading off, Margaret Mathews handing off to Wilma, and Isabelle Daniels running the anchor leg. Mae led the team with her motivational speeches and they were all ready to face the competition. Australia and Russia were favored to win. All the Tigerbelle handoffs were clean and the Americans finished third to claim the bronze medal, behind Australia and Great Britain. Australia won their fourth gold medal in the track events with their world record setting time of 44.5 seconds in the relay. Any disappointment over not doing well in the 200-meter race was washed away for Wilma. And while the relay team would have liked to win gold, they were glad to have run fast enough to win a medal. The four Tigerbelles stood on the victory stand happy with their bronze medals around their necks.

The Tigerbelle relay wrote a letter to Coach Temple on their flight back to the United States. In their letter, they recounted the details of their race to their coach. "There were only six medals gotten in the women's competition for the U.S.A., and we are truly proud to say that five of them were gotten by Tennessee State girls. We are even prouder (our relay) to bring home to you a world record. Everyone was surprised to learn that you coached all of us. The Australian team ran a 44.5, the British team ran a 44.7, and Tennessee State's team ran a 44.9. It was the first time in the history of the games that three teams broke the world's record in the same event. Maybe we could have been faster, but...we were more proud to get our bronze medal than the first two teams were to their medals. We really stood high on those steps." One of the signatures was by "Wilma 'Skeeter' Rudolph (your future star)."[30]

Mildred McDaniel won the only gold medal by an American woman at the 1956 Olympic Games in the high jump setting a world record with a jump of 5 feet 9 1/2 inches. Isabelle Daniels just missed winning a medal when she finished in 4th place in the 100-meter race. Willye

White finished second in the long jump, winning the silver medal with an American record leap of 19 feet and 11 1/2 inches. After the Olympic Games, Mae Faggs was the only female athlete invited by the U.S. State Department to travel overseas on a goodwill tour. These goodwill tours were another Cold War strategy used by the U.S. government to present American race relations by showcasing successful African American athletes. When she retired at age 24, Mae had at one point in her career held records, indoor and outdoor, in the 100-yard race, 220-yard race, 60-yard race, and the 4x100-meter, 4x100-yard, and 4x200-meter relays, and had helped establish the foundation for the Tennessee State Tigerbelle tradition.

As the Olympic Games wrapped up, teammates and competitors exchanged sweatshirts, shirts, and souvenirs and ended the trip with the closing ceremonies. Wilma was excited for the next Olympic Games in 1960, but was also excited to get back to high school and the upcoming basketball season in Clarksville, Tennessee. When she got back to Clarksville, Burt High School was closed for the day to host a special welcome home assembly for Wilma Rudolph, their hometown hero. After the assembly, Wilma found Coach Gray and told him she would be ready for the first game of the season, that very same night!

NOTES

1. In 1955, 9 of the 16 American women competing in the Pan-American Games in Mexico City were Black.

2. Susan Cahn, *Coming on Strong: Gender and Sexuality in Twentieth-Century Women's Sports* (New York: The Free Press, 1994), 131.

3. Cahn, *Coming on Strong,* 130.

4. This type of propaganda will be discussed further in chapter 11.

5. Mary Snow, "Can the Soviet Girls Be Stopped?" *Sports Illustrated,* August 27, 1956, 10.

6. Snow, "Can the Soviet Girls Be Stopped?" 10.

7. Snow, "Can the Soviet Girls Be Stopped?" 10–11.

8. Cahn, *Coming on Strong,* 120.

9. Cahn, *Coming on Strong,* 120.

10. According to Rita Liberti, Stokes finished 3rd in the 100-meter dash at the Olympic Trials earning her spot on the relay. See Rita Liberti, "Louise Stokes," in *African Americans in Sport: Volume 2,* ed. David K. Wiggins (Armonk, NY: M.E. Sharpe, 2004), 348.

11. Wrynn, "Tidye Pickett," in *African Americans in Sport: Volume 2,* ed. David K. Wiggins (Armonk, NY: M.E. Sharpe, 2004), 282.

12. A similar slight would occur at the 1936 Olympic Games in Berlin. Two Jewish American sprinters, Sam Stoll and Marty Glickman, were removed from the 4x100 meter relay and replaced with two African American runners, one of which was Jesse Owens. The relay gold was Owens fourth of the Games and established Owens as an "American" hero whose athletic success at the Games repudiated Adolf Hitler's theories of racial supremacy. For more on the 1936 Olympic Games, see Richard Mandell, *The Nazi Olympics*. For more on Jesse Owens, see William Baker, *Jesse Owens: An American Life* (New York: The Free Press).

13. Michael D. Davis, *Black American Women in Olympic Track and Field* (Jefferson, NC: McFarland & Company, 1992), 131.

14. According to Alison Wrynn, Pickett's foot caught a hurdle and she fell, breaking her shoulder, and effectively ending her track career. Wrynn states that the fall did not occur in the finals, but the semifinals. See Wrynn, "Tidye Pickett," in *African Americans in Sport: Volume 2*, ed. David K. Wiggins (Armonk, NY: M.E. Sharpe, 2004), 282.

15. Liberti, "Louise Stokes," 348.

16. Cindy Himes Gissendanner, "African American Women Olympians: The Impact of Race, Gender, and Class Ideologies, 1932–1968," *Research Quarterly for Exercise and Sport* 67 (2): 172–82, provides a comprehensive overview of the 1932 and 1936 Olympic experiences of Pickett and Stokes.

17. Cahn, *Coming on Strong*, 120.

18. Cahn, *Coming on Strong*, 125.

19. Cahn, *Coming on Strong*, 125–26.

20. Davis, *Black American Women in Olympic Track and Field*, 45.

21. Scoreboard, *Sports Illustrated*, September 3, 1956, 40–41.

22. Wilma Rudolph, *Wilma: The Story of Wilma Rudolph* (New York: Signet, 1977), 87.

23. Davis, *Black American Women*, 101–5.

24. Davis, *Black American Women*, 47–49.

25. Davis, *Black American Women*, 149–56.

26. Rudolph, *Wilma*, 89.

27. Rudolph, *Wilma*, 90.

28. Rudolph, *Wilma*, 95.

29. In her autobiography, Wilma says that she finished third in the semifinals, but that only the top two advanced, but if only the top two advanced from the semifinals, the finals would have four competitors instead of eight. She was most likely eliminated in the heat prior to the semifinals. See Rudolph, *Wilma*, 96.

30. Dwight Lewis and Susan Thomas, *A Will to Win* (Mt. Juliet, TN: Cumberland Press, 1983), 107.

Chapter 5

COMING HOME
TO BURT HIGH SCHOOL

After an exciting summer running at the Tennessee State Tigerbelles summer program and at the Olympics in Australia representing her country, Wilma returned to Clarksville, and was eager to get back on the basketball court for her junior season. She had seen the world outside Clarksville and liked what she saw. She even had a bronze medal to show for her Olympic efforts!

Wilma brought her medal to school to show her classmates. Of her return to Burt High School after her Olympic adventure, Wilma remembered the school hanging a "Welcome Home Wilma" banner and her classmates passing her medal around in admiration. When she returned home with her medal it had fingerprints all over it. She says of that day, "I took it and started shining it up. I discovered that bronze doesn't shine. So, I decided, I'm going to try this one more time. I'm going to go for the gold."[1] Of course, expectations for Wilma were raised because she had just participated in the world's biggest sporting competition. She did not let Clarksville down.

During Wilma's junior year, the basketball team had one of the best seasons in Tennessee history, even scoring over 100 points in a game. She remembered averaging 35 points a game, while her teammate Nancy Bowen also continued to score, averaging around 38 points per game. The team made it to the state tournament for the second year in a row and was determined to do better than they had the season before. The games were in Nashville again, and the team won all their games leading up to the final matchup with Merry High School, the alma mater of Coach Gray. Coach Gray really wanted to beat his former high school, and the team was motivated to win the title for their coach. Burt High School won the game in the final seconds even though according to Wilma's account of the game she had thrown the ball away at the end giving the Merry team a chance to win. Even after Burt won, Coach Gray was so upset about Wilma's turnover, he yelled at her turning the victory celebration into a bittersweet memory. Despite her success as an international Olympic athlete, Wilma was a teenager and still quite sensitive. She was especially sensitive to the criticism she felt Coach Gray expressed in front of her teammates and had a difficult time with his outbursts.

Repeating the seasonal pattern she had practiced now for several years, as soon as basketball season ended Wilma was ready to start running track, though she was also spending a good deal of time making up school work she had missed during her Olympic travels.[2] After establishing herself as an international athlete competing in the Olympics, Wilma felt that people had higher expectations of her in basketball, track, and everything she did. In fact, in many of her races that season, some girls refused to even run against her because she was so good. She was frustrated and felt that when they did run against her they didn't even seem to try to beat her. She won every race that season. Track and field at the high school level was still relatively unorganized and for an accomplished athlete like Wilma, it was relatively easy to be successful against much weaker competitors. For Wilma to get any competition on the track, she was going to have to wait for the summer with the Tigerbelles.

At the end of her junior year of high school, Wilma was excited to attend the school prom. Not having enough money for a dress, Shirley Crowder, a Tigerbelle Wilma had become friends with at Tennessee State, lent her a blue prom dress. Wilma's date was her steady boyfriend, Robert Eldridge. Robert played on the basketball and football teams, and Wilma thought of herself with Robert as the King and Queen of Burt High School. Prom night was full of excitement; Robert borrowed his father's Ford, Wilma tried smoking a cigarette in the bathroom, and it was the end of the school year! In her autobiography, Wilma remembers her prom night as her first encounter with tragedy. After the prom, Wilma and her friends drove 25 miles away to Hopkinsville, Kentucky, to a club that would serve them alcohol. They raced to Hopkinsville and after hanging out there for about an hour, a fight broke out. They decided to leave and someone yelled, "Last one to Clarksville is a chicken." They returned to Clarksville and Wilma ended up spending the night at her teammate Delma's house. She and Delma were awakened by a phone call at around four in the morning by Coach Gray, who informed them that their teammate Nancy Bowen had been killed in a car accident driving back from Kentucky. Wilma was stunned and saddened. Nancy had been one of Wilma's best friends and basketball teammate. Her death was difficult for Wilma to comprehend, and she found refuge in running with the Tigerbelles throughout the summer.

Wilma left Clarksville at the end of the school year and headed back to Tennessee State in Nashville to train with Coach Temple and the Tigerbelles. Still shocked by the loss of her friend, being at Tennessee State and training hard helped her to deal with her feelings.

Wilma spent the summer of 1957, her third in a row, at Tennessee State training with Coach Temple and his Tigerbelles. At the national outdoor AAU championships in Cleveland, Ohio, Wilma set new girls' division AAU records in three events, the 75-yard dash, the 100-yard dash, and the 300-yard relay.[3] These were Wilma's first AAU records of her career, and it was a great motivation for her as she entered her final year of high school.

Wilma was ready for her senior year in high school and pumped up for her final seasons in basketball and track. Her relationship with Robert was getting more serious and she admitted that she was in love with him. Getting ready for basketball, she was required to take a physical exam. The doctor informed her that she was pregnant and Wilma was shocked. Wilma's religious upbringing had made the topic of sex a taboo subject with her mother. She did not feel like she could tell her parents about the pregnancy and admitted that, as a teenager, she had been naïve about sex and contraceptives. She was equally afraid of what Coach Temple would do when he found out. She didn't tell anyone of her pregnancy for a few weeks.

One day in practice Coach Gray yelled at her for being lazy and gaining weight. He went to the doctor and asked about Wilma's condition. Though the doctor did not tell Coach Gray that Wilma was pregnant, the coach realized she was and told her that her health was more important than basketball. She was "mortified" about her pregnancy and recalled not being able to really understand the situation. She had just starting having sex with Robert and ended up pregnant. She and Robert were both very innocent and naïve about sex. Neither had anticipated that their intimacy would result in Wilma getting pregnant. Wilma finally confided in her older sister Yvonne, who helped to break the news to her mother who then told her father. In the meantime, Wilma's boyfriend and the father of her baby, Robert, had started dating another girl, which was very upsetting for Wilma. Wilma's parents were somewhat understanding about her pregnancy, although they forbid her from seeing Robert. Her father told her, "Don't worry about anything, don't be ashamed of anything, everybody makes mistakes."[4] There was never any talk of Wilma having an abortion, which was illegal in Tennessee at the time, or of sending her away until she had the baby, which was a common practice for White teenage girls during this time period. According to Wilma, "There were lots of other girls in that school in the same condition that I was in, and there really wasn't any stigma to it at all."[5] Wilma stayed at Burt High School and finished her senior year as an expectant mother. Basketball and track were out of the question. Her life had changed dramatically in less than a year, and her future plans of attending college were in question.

The one person who had yet to hear the news about Wilma's pregnancy was Coach Temple. When Coach Temple finally heard the news, he drove straight to Wilma's house to meet with her and her parents. As a policy, Coach Temple did not recruit girls to run at Tennessee State who had babies. He visited with Wilma and her parents to discuss the situation and informed them that he would break this rule, because he still wanted Wilma to attend Tennessee State after she finished high school. This was a great relief to Wilma and her parents, who wanted their daughter to attend college and continue running track. Wilma continued to attend school pregnant and graduated from Burt High School in May 1958. Two months later, in July, Wilma gave birth to her daughter, Yolanda.[6]

Having a baby as a teenage mother was not an ideal situation, but Wilma was fortunate to have the support of her family and Coach Temple. Many accounts of Wilma's life do not mention her pregnancy, but indicate that she was ill as a senior in high school and unable to compete in sports. It is not clear where such stories originated, but Wilma, in her own accounts of her life was forthcoming about the birth of her first child and the stress of becoming a mother at a young age when her concerns were more focused on running fast. Despite not competing in basketball or track during her senior year and not being able to attend Coach Temple's summer program for the first time in four years, Wilma still planned on attending college at Tennessee State. She also missed out on running for the American team at the Pan American Games and the United States versus the Soviet Union competitions during the summer of 1958. However, not only would she have the opportunity to run track again, Wilma would receive a college education, something no one in her family had done before. Wilma's family vowed to care for baby Yolanda while she was in school. Wilma still had dreams of returning to the Olympics and winning a gold medal, and Tennessee State was the place that would help to achieve her dreams.

NOTES

1. Anne Janette Johnson, *Great Women in Sports* (Detroit: Visible Ink Press, 1996), 407.

2. According to Davis, Rudolph did not run seriously after the Olympics until she returned to Tennessee State in the summer of 1957. Wilma, however, recalled in her autobiography, running track her junior year. While high school track was still relatively unorganized, it would have been possible for her to run in some meets and not others. See Michael D. Davis, *Black American Women in Olympic Track and Field* (Jefferson, NC: McFarland & Company, Inc., 1992), 114.

3. Davis, *Black American Women*, 114.

4. Wilma Rudolph, with Martin Ralbovsky, *Wilma: The Story of Wilma Rudolph* (New York: Signet, 1977), 111.

5. Rudolph, *Wilma*, 112.

6. Several sources indicate that Wilma did not compete in 1958 because she was injured, but in fact she did not compete because she was pregnant and then recovering from childbirth.

Chapter 6

BECOMING
A TENNESSEE STATE TIGERBELLE

After graduating from Burt High School in 1958, Wilma was awarded a full scholarship to attend Tennessee State University in Nashville where she would run for Coach Temple as an official Tigerbelle. Her scholarship was financial aid that required her to work on campus to earn the scholarship money, which is very different from the athletic scholarships available to female athletes today. Wilma had not run track since the summer before her senior year due to her pregnancy, but she had been preparing to be one of Coach Temple's full-fledged Tennessee State Tigerbelles since her first summer at Tennessee State in 1955. Robert had asked Wilma to marry him and start a family together, but Wilma's father was against it and still blamed him for getting Wilma pregnant. Her family wanted Wilma to receive a college education and continue her track career, hopefully making the team for the next Olympic Games.

Wilma was excited to be a Tigerbelle and was determined to qualify for the 1960 Olympics. She knew that attending Tennessee State would help her achieve this goal. It was still a difficult decision, because Wilma's father was very sick making it impossible for her mother to take care of baby Yolanda. Wilma realized it would have been very difficult for her to attend college, run track, and take care of her daughter. She arranged for her older sister Yvonne, in St. Louis, to take care of baby Yolanda so she could attend college and run track. By the end of her freshman year, Wilma's mother decided she could take care of Yolanda. Coach Temple was not willing to bend any rules to make life easier for Wilma and was a strict disciplinarian, which meant she did not get to make trips home to Clarksville to visit her family and child as often as she would have liked to.

Tennessee Agricultural & Industrial State Normal School for Negroes opened in September 1912 to 247 students.[1] That same year, the school fielded their first football team. The school served as the first summer school for African American educators in Tennessee, which was the last segregated state to build a public college for its African American citizens. The university was established as a college to train students to earn their teaching credentials to teach at the elementary and secondary levels. In 1925, the school changed their name to Tennessee A&I State Normal College and in 1927, dropped the word Normal from their title. Soon a graduate school was added and by the 1940s, enrollment was close to 1,500 students. In 1951, the school name was changed to Tennessee A&I State University, but would commonly be referred to as Tennessee State University or Tennessee State.

Tennessee State's women were well represented on the 1956 Olympic team, with the majority of the nine African American women coming from the Tennessee State track team. Tennessee State, a historically Black college, along with Tuskegee, presented Black women an opportunity to receive an education and participate in sport. These historically Black colleges were "pioneers in competitive sport opportunities for women long before the women's movement."[2] When Coach Temple was asked about the problems of fielding a good women's team, he answered with, "We have to take an American girl with her powder and lipstick and develop her into a competitor. She has to be feminine and talented. This combination is hard to find."[3] Despite the rising success of American women in track and field, the sport was still considered masculine and was marginalized in the sporting press, save for every four years with the Olympic Games bringing interest and attention to the sport. Temple, as part of his coaching responsibilities, felt he had the task of insuring that his women would not do anything to perpetuate the negative stereotypes about track and field and the masculinity of the participating women. For example, he instituted a dress code and would not allow the women to be photographed after a race until they had showered and changed into dress clothes.

By the time Wilma enrolled at Tennessee State in the fall of 1958, Coach Temple and the Tigerbelles were on top of the track and field world. African American women were dominating international track and field and were America's best chances against their Soviet counterparts. In 1957, at the AAU outdoor nationals, six Tigerbelles ran against each other in the finals of the 200-meter race. The next year, there were 10 Tigerbelles on scholarship, and all 10 qualified for the

Pan-American Games team. That same year, Coach Temple led a team of American women, including seven Tigerbelles (Barbara Jones, Lucinda Williams, Margaret Mathews, Willye White, Martha Hudson, Annie Lois Smith, and Isabelle Daniels) on a European tour of track meets to Moscow, Warsaw, Budapest, and Athens.[4] Wilma missed out on the European competitions because she had just given birth to her daughter and was not able to run. Historian Susan Cahn explained that "by presenting a public image of well-dressed feminine composure, black sports advocates insisted in integrating African American athletes into standards of athletic femininity. This approach continued a tradition of African American resistance in which generations of black women had defended their femininity and sexual virtue against disparaging stereotypes by asserting their morality and respectability."[5] Perhaps these ideas influenced Coach Temple's policy of not allowing his athletes to have children.

Only a few years prior, *Ebony* magazine had stated that Black female athletes owed their success to their male coaches, explaining that the lady tracksters' performances could never match those of their male counterparts. The magazine concluded that boys were learning "that a girl track star can be as feminine as the china-doll type."[6] Cahn suggests that "when, after decades of media and organizational neglect, American track women suddenly found themselves under the international glare of Cold War athletic rivalries, a complicated matrix of racial and gender issues came to a head. A reservoir of racist beliefs about black women being deficient in femininity buttressed the masculine connotation of track and field. Throughout the Cold War era, the sport was dominated by African American and Soviet women. Thus two symbols of mannishness—black women and Russian 'amazons'—stood in the foreground, impeding efforts to overhaul the sport's reputation."[7] Under the glare of Cold War politics, African American female athletes enjoyed greater media attention and accolades, but at a price that compromised both their race and gender. On one hand, they faced racism from an American society divided by race and still segregated in schools, public facilities, and daily practices. On the other hand, they faced sexism in an American society that devalued their athletic accomplishments in a male dominated sport world, as well as expectations of females and femininity.

The dominance of African American women in track and field posed a problem for American promoters and sport advocates trying to revive "popular interest in a dying sport." Cahn states that track and field promoters had two choices to help the sport; they could "incorporate black track women into approved concepts of athletic womanhood" or they could "minimize the presence and contributions of black women in order to create a more respectable image of the sport."[8] It seemed clear that keeping African American women out of the sport would be difficult; they were America's best hopes for winning medals!

Coach Temple bought into the prescribed images for Black women in sport and did his best to help soften their image to fit into the accepted ideals of femininity. Temple explained, "None of my girls have any trouble getting boyfriends. I tell them that they are young ladies first, track girls second."[9] His strategy paid off in many ways. One of the first lessons a Tigerbelle learned was that she was "a lady first" and a "track lady second." Another one of Temple's sayings was "I don't want oxes, I want foxes." Years later he explained his philosophy. "I wanted nice looking girls who took care of themselves who could also run. I had it in mind that if we went someplace, I wanted a stranger to wonder, 'What do you young ladies do? Do you sing or are you a debating team?' I wanted this because at that time, there was a real dilemma over women participating in sports. People used to say that if the girls got muscles they could never have babies. I was determined to overcome that kind of stuff. I was going to prove to the world that you could be feminine and still get the job done."[10] To help achieve this Temple instituted three rules; his runners had to complete their college education, they had to be on time for everything, and there was a strictly defined coach–athlete relationship.

Davis marks this Tigerbelle era as an important break from the previous images of women's track stars, which had been viewed as "muscular, masculine women."[11] To some Americans, having a child, as Wilma had done, confirmed her femininity and womanhood at a time when it was in question for many African American female athletes. At the same time, however, it reinforced ideas about poor Black females having children at too young an age. Wilma's role as a mother was never used to promote a feminine image in track. Perhaps because she bore her daughter without being married, which at the time did not fit into traditional ideas about family, femininity, and motherhood.

It was into this world of conflicting views on womanhood and athleticism that Wilma entered college as a mother and international athlete. She was no longer a high school runner at Coach Temple's summer program, she was a college athlete and an official Tennessee State Tigerbelle. This move to the college level was significant and carried new responsibilities. Coach Temple was very demanding on his athletes and made the athletes run an extra lap for every minute they were late to practice. Rudolph once overslept practice by 30 minutes and had to run 30 extra laps. The next day she was sitting on the track 30 minutes early.

Adjusting to college life was difficult for Wilma, especially balancing school work and running track. She was majoring in elementary education and had a minor in psychology. She had to keep up good grades to stay on the team. She frequently lost to her teammates and was frustrated with her inconsistent performances. At times, balancing everything was a challenge and Wilma considered quitting school until one day one of her professors, Mr. Knight, asked her to consider two things. First, he reminded her that her baby was in good hands with her family. He also pressed her to consider all the sacrifices she had made for track and wondered if she was really willing to throw all her hard work away. Wilma credits that conversation with her decision to stick things out and stay in school.

Wilma was surrounded by talented teammates, some of who had been her Olympic teammates, such as Margaret Mathews, Lucinda Williams, Isabelle Daniels, and Willye White. Margaret Mathews spoke to the conflicts the women faced when it came to the issue of femininity; "I found out you don't have to be pretty to be recognized, to be known, to be somebody. Some people are partial; some people like pretty people, attractive people. Others, if you have the talent, it doesn't matter; and that's how it was with Mrs. Morgan [her physical education teacher and coach]. She was never partial; she always gave us an equal chance and I think that's what gave me the incentive to really want to be somebody."[12] She was referring to her high school coach Marian Armstrong-Perkins, who had been a chaperone for the Tigerbelle summer program and several U.S. women's teams. Willye White also admitted the tensions she felt as a female athlete; "It is pretty difficult being all female, you know, because you are out there on the track and you're in all the dirt and grime and grit doing the same thing the boys are doing, and you don't carry yourself as feminine as some girls would. You're not as dainty as they are because most times your feet hurt, you have sore muscles, and it's pretty difficult to be all woman out on the track. This is something that you just can't be; you gotta let yourself go, whereas the average women is constantly fixing her makeup or combing her hair and trying to look pretty. Well, when you're out on the track with makeup and you start sweating, it smears; and that makes you look worse. So what you do is your hard work and you look ugly out on the track and after the track meet is over you come back, fix yourself up, and then you're a pretty lady."[13] Just as Coach Temple had his rules about postrace interviews and the appearance of his athletes, the Tigerbelles were also cognizant of the pressures they faced to appear feminine.

In addition to her 1956 Olympic teammates, other talented Tigerbelles running with Wilma at Tennessee State included Shirley Crowder and Barbara Jones. Shirley was from Temple, Georgia, and graduated from Booker T. Washington High School. Shirley, who a year earlier had lent Wilma her blue prom dress, did not make the 1956 Olympics team because she tripped over a hurdle at the Olympic Trials. Shirley, however, did win the 80-meter hurdle championship at the AAU outdoor meet in 1957.[14] Wilma and Shirley first met in the summer of 1955 when they both attended Coach Temple's summer program. Like Wilma, Shirley had been a star basketball player in high school.

Barbara Jones, also a Tigerbelle, had won a gold medal in the 4x100-meter relay for the United States in the 1952 Olympic Games. Barbara grew up in the South Side of Chicago and had run for the Catholic Youth Organization in Chicago. When she lost to three Tigerbelles at the 1956 Olympic Trials in the 100-meter race and failed to qualify for the Olympic team, Mae Faggs told her "The thing you need to do is come down to Tennessee State and learn what training is all about."[15] So she did.

Running on the Tigerbelle track team was going well for Wilma. Wilma thought that she was even faster after having her baby. Still, she routinely lost races to her teammates and was inconsistent in her performances during her freshman and sophomore years due to injuries and illnesses. She finally was examined by a doctor and had a tonsillectomy. The tonsil infection had been bothering her for months and made training difficult. After the surgery, she regained her old form.

As a freshman in college, Wilma won the 50-yard dash in 6.2 seconds at the National Indoor AAU Track Championship held at Washington, D.C.'s National Guard Armory and was a leg of the second place 440-yard relay to help Tennessee State, with 61 1/2 total points, win the title easily over second place finishers, the Queen Mercurettes of New York and the Police Athletic League of New York, both with a mere 18 points.[16] In the summer of 1959, Wilma won the AAU title in the 100-yard dash. During her sophomore season, Wilma set two American records at the indoor AAU championships held in Chicago in April 1960 leading Tennessee State to their sixth consecutive national indoor title. She won the 50-yard dash, and set records in the 100-yard dash (11.1 seconds) and 220-yard dash (25.7 seconds), breaking former teammate Mae Faggs' 220-yard record of 25.9 seconds established in 1959.[17]

Coach Temple was selected as the head coach for the women's track team 1958 and 1959 competitions between the United States and the Soviet Union, the 1959 Pan-American Games, and the 1960 Olympic Games. Eight Tigerbelles competed for the United States at the 1959

Philadelphia American-Soviet meet, and 10 Tigerbelles ran at the 1959 Pan-American Games, including Wilma. At the American-Soviet dual meet in Philadelphia, Wilma finished third in the 100-meter dash to her teammate Barbara Jones. At the Pan-American Games, Wilma's relay set a new meet record, though the real star of the meet was teammate Lucinda Williams, who, in addition to running on the relay, won the 100-meter dash and the 200-meter dash.[18]

Wilma's goals were focused on making the 1960 Olympic track and field team and winning more medals, with hopes for a gold medal. The first step to meeting this goal was to perform well at the National AAU meet held in Corpus Christi, Texas. The best runners at the AAU meet would be invited to the Olympic Trials to be held a couple of weeks later at Texas Christian University. Wilma was set on qualifying in several events. Years later, two incidents stayed in Wilma's mind from the Nationals that year. First, her youngest sister, Charlene, the baby of the Rudolph family, was also scheduled to run, but became very sick. The second incident involved a bus driver who refused to drive the integrated American track team and walked off leaving the athletes to wait for another driver. Wilma and her teammates eventually made it to the meet and Wilma met several of her immediate goals, qualifying for several events at the Olympic Trials. She repeated her AAU title in the 100-yard dash. She was definitely ready for the Olympic Trials.

At the Olympic Trials, Wilma competed in the 100-meter and 200-meter races and the 4x100-meter relay. In the 200-meter race final, Wilma set a world record running a blazing 22.9 seconds to win and became the first American woman to hold a world record in a running event. Her record would stand for five years.[19] Coach Temple did not tell her about the record. Later that day, she found out from her teammates and celebrated both her world record and making her second Olympic team in all three events—the 100-meter and 200-meter dashes, and the 400-meter relay.

Those who had earned a spot on the Olympic team moved on to train at Kansas State University in Emporia, Kansas, just like they had done in Los Angeles four years earlier. The facilities in Emporia were top rate. This time, the coach of the team was none other than the Tigerbelle's own Ed Temple, who had several of his runners on the Olympic team. Fran Welch, the head coach at Emporia State College, was Coach Temple's assistant coach for the Olympics. They practiced three times a day the first week, cutting back to twice a day the second week, eventually practicing once a day during the last week of training. There were 18 women on the Olympic team; 11 of them were African American, and 8 of those 11 were from Tennessee State.

Wilma headed to the Games in Rome, Italy, that summer expecting to win three gold medals. She wrote, "Everything was in place for me, and all I had to do was deliver my end of it."[20] Not everyone expected her to win three medals, however, least of all her teammates, who routinely beat her and were outstanding athletes hoping to win their own Olympic medals.

NOTES

1. Dwight Lewis and Susan Thomas, *A Will to Win* (Mt. Juliet, TN: Cumberland Press, 1983), 2.

2. Yevonne R. Smith, "Women of Color in Society and Sport," *Quest* (August 1992), 236–37.

3. Events and Discoveries, *Sports Illustrated*, 15 September 1958.

4. This would have been the summer of 1958. Wilma was not on the Pan-American team because she was unable to compete spending most of her senior year pregnant.

5. Susan Cahn, *Coming on Strong: Gender and Sexuality in Twentieth-Century Women's Sport* (New York: The Free Press, 1994), 134.

6. Cahn, *Coming on Strong*, 134.

7. Cahn, *Coming on Strong*, 138.

8. Cahn, *Coming on Strong*, 133.

9. Cahn, *Coming on Strong*, 133.

10. Lewis and Thomas, *A Will to Win*, 116–17.

11. Michael D. Davis, *Black American Women in Olympic Track and Field* (Jefferson, NC: McFarland & Company, Inc., 1992), 80.

12. Davis, *Black American Women*, 102.

13. Davis, *Black American Women*, 155–56.

14. Davis, *Black American Women*, 46–47.

15. Davis, *Black American Women*, 79.

16. "Tennessee A. and I. Women Gain National Indoor Track Crown," *New York Times*, 25 January 1959, S1.

17. "Wilma Rudolph Sets 2 Records," *New York Times*, 17 April 1960, S7.

18. Davis, *Black American Women*, 116.

19. Davis, *Black American Women*, 117.

20. Wilma Rudolph, with Martin Ralbovsky, *Wilma: The Story of Wilma Rudolph* (New York: Signet, 1977), 124.

Wilma Rudolph competed at the 1960 Olympic Games. This was her second Olympics, but it was the first time the games were televised around the world. This gave Wilma and her teammates increased media exposure. Library of Congress.

Wilma stands with her 1960 Olympic gold medal 4x100m relay teammates, Lucinda Williams, Barbara Jones, and Martha Hudson. Library of Congress.

Wilma enjoys welcome home celebrations with her parents, Blanche and Ed Rudolph. Getty Images.

Wilma shows off her medals with fellow Olympian and Tennessee State classmate, Ralph Boston. Getty Images.

Wilma is victorious at Madison Square Garden with a world record time. 1960. Library of Congress.

Wilma talks with President John F. Kennedy at the White House. The President said that he was honored to meet an Olympian. 1961. Library of Congress.

Wilma is pictured here on the set of the TV movie "Wilma," with Piper Carter (who played Wilma, age 4). 1975. Photofest.

Chapter 7

WILMA RUNS TO HISTORY
AT THE 1960 OLYMPIC GAMES

Despite being overlooked by the American media, by Black male athletes, and by the sporting public, both Black and White—Black female athletes were largely responsible for the increasing improvement in status, ability, and power of the American track and field Olympic teams of the 1960s. Black men were dominating, in their athletic performances though not necessarily in numbers, a majority of professional sports, including baseball, football, basketball, boxing, and track. Track and field was the main recipient of the great talent these Black women had to offer. The lone exception to that pattern had been Althea Gibson, who was the first African American athlete to break the color barrier in tennis and won the U.S. Open title in 1957 and Wimbledon in 1957 and 1958. After Gibson's retirement from professional tennis in 1958, the visibility of African American women in sport beside track and field diminished significantly. Many believe that Gibson's stardom came a decade too early, as there were too few opportunities for women to earn a living playing tennis in the 1950s and 1960s. Gibson then joined the Ladies Professional Gold Association and began a singing career, though she struggled financially for much of her life. Though Gibson was the first African American female athlete to become an internationally famous female athlete, racism dogged her at every turn, even preventing her from competing in tournaments. In her 1958 autobiography, *I Always Wanted to Be Somebody*, Gibson admitted "I am not a racially conscious person. I don't want to be. I see myself as just an individual."[1] At the start of the new decade, integrated high profile athletics were still primarily the pursuit of men.

The 1960 Rome Olympic Games was a major event that highlighted the athletic achievements of African American females on the national and international stage. Press coverage of African American female athletes remained scarce in both White and Black newspapers, though exceptions did occur with the occasional Olympic victories and Wimbledon titles. The 1960 Rome Olympic Games marked the first time in Olympic history that the Games would be televised around the world making the athletic accomplishments accessible to the sporting public in a way that allowed the images and victories to spread faster than ever before. At these Games, Wilma Rudolph was one of a number of sporting personalities who seemed perfect for the medium of television.

Wilma was making her second appearance in the Olympic Games. After spending a week in New York City getting measured for Olympic uniforms, the U.S. team flew to Rome two weeks prior to the start of the Games. During those two weeks before the Games, Wilma was able to see the sights of Rome. She marveled at the Roman Coliseum, the catacombs, and the Vatican, home to the Pope. Her roommate for the Olympics was her Tigerbelle teammate and relay teammate, Lucinda Williams. The Olympic Village was smaller than the Village in Melbourne, and one thing that left an impression on Wilma was the cafeteria, where they could eat anytime they wanted. There was also a recreation hall where the athletes hung out together, and every night a dance was held. Just as they had been in Australia, the American athletes were very popular in the Olympic Village and there was quite a bit of international camaraderie. There were over 6,000 athletes from 84 countries. It was the last year that South Africa would be allowed to participate due to their apartheid policies in society and sport.[2] The Rome Organizing Committee had not only spent lavishly on the facilities, over $50 million, they also incorporated sites from Ancient Games, sporting competitions over 2,000 years earlier, like the Basilica of Maxentius for the wrestling events and the Terme di Caracalla for gymnastics.

As noted, the 1960 Olympic Games were being broadcast on televisions around the world which afforded Americans the opportunity to see Wilma and her teammates compete for the very first time. More and more Americans had television sets in their homes, albeit they were in black and white, and the Olympics were quickly becoming the largest international sport competition. The Games were televised in more than 100 countries, including a time delay in the United States, Canada, and Japan. Having the Games televised allowed the American public the opportunity to witness the athletic feats of their American athletes in a way that helped connect the public to the sporting competition. Unlike having to wait to read about an American victory in the next morning's newspaper or see the event on a movie reel months later, the televised coverage helped promote the sporting activities of both American male and female athletes. For many Americans, as well as people around the world, it was the first time seeing women compete in sport on television. Leading up to the Games, the Cold War rivalry between the United States and the Soviet Union resulted in an increased popularity of women's track and field. The dual meets between the powerhouses leading up to the Games also contributed to this growing interest in women's track and field. The television coverage of these Olympics only added to the popularity. In the 1960 Olympics, there were four new events for women competitors in track and field, along with the reinstatement of the 800-meter run. In 1928, the public could not accept images of female athletes so fatigued from running a half mile, and the reaction to the photographed images of the fallen runners marked the end of the distance events for women until the Olympic Games in Rome.

This was Wilma's second trip to the Olympics, and having Coach Temple as the head coach of the team was a benefit for Wilma, who felt relaxed and happy to have a familiar face at the biggest meet of her life. In fact, seven Tigerbelles were on the 1960 Olympic team.[3] Before she even competed in her first race, Coach Temple sat her down and told her about a recurring dream he had been having. In his dream, Wilma had won three gold medals becoming the first American woman to do so. His dreams only confirmed what Wilma had been feeling in practices—she was ready to run. Wilma had been upset that in a track newsletter circulating around the Village her name did not appear until the sixth page. Coach Temple said, "Don't worry about it, the news-letter doesn't mean anything; whoever put it together doesn't know anything."[4] He reminded her that she had been consistently running the 100 meters in 11.4 seconds and that none of the competition came close to her. That was all Wilma needed to hear from Coach Temple, who was a major source of comfort for Wilma and her Tennessee State teammates.

All was not going as smoothly as Coach Temple's dream. Just as Wilma had battled injuries and illnesses throughout her track career, the 1960 Olympic Games were no exception. During a practice leading up to her first race, Wilma sprained her ankle when she stepped into a hole. She was worried she might not be able to compete in any of her events and iced her ankle all day. When she woke up the next morning, the ankle was a little sore, but she knew she could run on it. As she entered the stadium, she felt a sense of calm nervousness, and reports that she knew deep inside that she could beat the other competitors. That day, in the 100-meter dash race, she won her first two heats. In one of her preliminary heats she had tied the world record running it in 11.3 seconds. It seemed that her ankle would not be slowing her down at all.

The next day she iced her ankle again and won the third heat and then the fourth heat. In the fourth heat, again she set a world record, running the 100-meters in 11 seconds. But the International Olympic Committee did not allow the world record to stand because the wind had been blowing too hard, 2.2 miles per hour, giving Wilma a push from behind. She was upset to not have the record, but glad to be advancing to the finals of the event with confidence. In the finals, Wilma had a good start and outsprinted Italy's Giuseppina Leone and Dorothy Hyman, of Great Britain, to win her first Olympic gold medal. Wilma ran a record 11 seconds again, but another ruling discounted the world record. Wilma Rudolph became the first American woman to win a gold medal in the 100-meters since Helen Stephens had done it in 1936. Wilma later said that she had won the race for American sprinter Ray Norton; it was rumored she was dating Ray, and she said his loss earlier that day spurned her on. She was heartsick when Ray lost in the men's 100-meter finals and thought that one way to cheer him up would be to win a gold medal for him. After she won, the sprinting couple left Stadio Olympico arm in arm. According to her calculations and expectations, she had one gold medal down, and two to go.

In Wilma's second race, the 200-meter race, she faced almost the same competitors as she did in the 100-meters. Her ankle was healing and she felt much better running the curves of the 200 meters. In the preliminary heats, she set an Olympic record in the 200 meters running it in 23.2 seconds. She was extremely confident in the race and felt that no one could beat her. No one could, and Wilma won her second gold medal of the Games in 24 seconds, with West Germany's Jutta Heine winning silver and Britain's Dorothy Hyman repeating her bronze medal performance. Wilma, however, was disappointed in her time; it was more than a second slower than her world record time, but she acknowledged that the strong wind had slowed her down a bit. Two gold medals down, one to go.

The 4x100-meter relay was the last race Wilma had left to run and the last medal she hoped to win. She was characterized by *Time* magazine as "the calmest person on the U.S. squad, contrasting sharply with her steady date, tense and tormented Sprinter Ray Norton." Discussing Wilma's pre-race mood, Coach Temple said, "There's not a nerve in her body. She's almost lazy. She often goes to sleep between the semifinal and final runs. The she gets over those starting blocks and—boom—all that harnessed energy explodes into speed."[5]

On September 7, 1960, over 60,000 spectators sat in Rome's Stadio Olympico to watch Wilma and her teammates run in the finals of the relay. She would be running the anchor leg with Martha Hudson, Barbara Jones, and Lucinda Williams rounding out the relay foursome. All four women were Tigerbelles. The United States faced tough competition from West Germany, Russia, and Great Britain. According to Temple's account of the relay, there was some trouble leading up to the handoff between Lucinda and Wilma. Temple recalled, "The baton was bobbled when Lucinda passed off to Rudolph. My heart sank to my feet. That one bobble gave Germany and Australia enough time to pull ahead and put us in third place. Rudolph accelerated quickly and passed the two front runners in the first fifteen yards. She was so determined that I don't believe anyone could have stopped her. When she broke the tape, she became the first American woman ever to win three gold medals in the Olympics."[6] Despite the fumbling of the baton handoff, Wilma was able to catch up and pass the Soviet Union's anchor leg, Irina Press, in the final stretch of the race in a time of 44.5 seconds, close to their world record performance of 44.4 seconds they had run in the semifinals. Wilma Rudolph had made history. She was the first American woman to win three Olympic gold medals in track and field and was the only track and field athlete, male or female, to win three gold medals at the 1960 Olympic Games in Rome. Her hometown newspaper, the Clarksville *Leaf-Chronicle* said she was "an inspiration to the world in general" and Tennessee's Governor Buford Ellington, who had run for office as an "old fashioned segregationist," was making plans for a welcome home party.[7]

Wilma had become the darling of the Rome Olympics; one official told her life would never be the same. Wilma said she felt some "animosity" from some of her teammates who felt like she was getting all the attention and recognition. She felt like she had earned the recognition—after all, she had just won three gold medals, something no American woman had ever done before in track and field![8] Years later, Wilma admitted "I think everybody that goes to the Olympics thinks inside that they're going to win. And regardless of whether you win or not, you have to believe there is some possibility. My goal was to go to the 1960 Olympics and win one of something. You never think you're going to win everything. There is just something about being there. There's the traveling and everything. The key motivator is just the conglomeration of being involved in the Olympics."[9] Wilma was reminded of the conversations she had with Mae Faggs four year earlier when the senior Tigerbelle told her to run her fastest and not to worry about pleasing her teammates. One teammate who was not jealous of Wilma and who remained a supportive friend to her during the 1960 Games was Earlene Brown, a shot putter and discus thrower, who had also been one of Wilma's teammates at the 1956 Games. Though Earlene was not a Tigerbelle, the two athletes hit it off and enjoyed each other's company.

Growing up in California, Earlene's early sporting accomplishments were in the basketball throw, which was an event that led up to the shot put.[10] Like Wilma, she was a young mother and had given birth to her son Reggie before she had ever competed in a national meet. A hairdresser, Earlene struggled financially which made training difficult. She did not attend college, which meant that she had to pay for all her training expenses as well as traveling to track meets. Earlene was a crowd favorite everywhere she went and helped Wilma adjust to fame; "Signing autographs is the key to your popularity, because a lot of them [athletes] don't want to be bothered by little people. I enjoy it. I always did. Lots of times Wilma and I would get caught signing autographs. Once you stopped to sign one, you could look to get tied up, and you just kept signing until you signed yourself right into the gate at Olympic Village."[11] A special friendship existed between Earlene and Wilma. Earlene often helped comb Wilma's hair to make she sure looked good for the press. At the 1960 Games, Earlene finished third in the shot put with a throw of 53 feet 10 1/4 inches. She finished sixth in the discus throw.

Wilma's Tigerbelle teammates enjoyed varying levels of success at the Games including her relay teammates, Barbara Jones, who was eliminated in the 100-meter dash; Lucinda Williams, who did not reach the finals in the 100-meter or 200-meter dash; and Martha Hudson, had only run the relay for gold. Shirley Crowder ran the 80-meter hurdles, but did not reach the finals. Willye White could not match her silver medal performance of four years earlier and finished a disappointing 16th place. High jumper Neomia Rodgers finished a disappointing 14th place, but had the best jump of her life. Mildred White, her physical education teacher, discovered Neomia's athletic abilities and persuaded her family to let their daughter train at Tuskegee Institute's summer program. Neomia was the daughter of a one-legged sharecropper from Roba, Alabama, and had attended Macon County Training School; the only one of 11 children to finish school.

Overall, America had finished second, behind the powerful Soviet Union and one ahead of Italy, in the unofficial total medal count. The Soviet Union had tallied a total of 103 medals with 43 gold medals, while the United States had accumulated a total of 71 medals with 34 accounting for gold. There were notable performances by other American athletes at the Games besides Rudolph, including 18-year-old Cassius Clay, who later became known as Muhammad Ali, who won a gold medal in the light heavyweight division in boxing, along with Rafer Johnson, who was the gold medalist in the decathlon. Johnson had carried the American flag in the opening ceremonies and many wondered if that patriotic honor motivated his tremendous athletic performance in his event.

One American athlete who had been expected to do well was the sprinter romantically linked to Wilma, Ray Norton. Norton was expected to win the 100-meter and 200-meter races, and 400-meter relays, just like Wilma, but he finished sixth in both the sprints. In the relay the U.S. men's team was disqualified when Norton ran out of the baton exchange zone.[12] Only a few weeks after the Games, Wilma was seen in New York City wearing a diamond engagement ring, but she explained that it belonged to her mother, and refused to comment on reports that she and Norton were planning to get married. She did say she had "a fellow in mind and he likes running, too."[13] Still, nothing came of the budding romance between Ray and Wilma, but it certainly was fun for newspaper reporters to write about!

Press coverage of Wilma's accomplishments at the Olympic Games largely focused on her appearance, related to both femininity and skin color. She was often compared to a gazelle, which has been critiqued as a way to suggest that the athlete was "animal like," though the newspapers explained it was about her grace and speed. The European press loved Wilma Rudolph, and each country's newspapers had their own nicknames for her. The French called Wilma "La Gazelle," "La Chattanooga Choo Choo," and "La Perle Noir" (the black pearl). The Italians called her "La Gazella Nera" (the black gazelle). Rudolph, unlike her African American team-mates, was described by her skin color. The American press described her as a "cafe au lait runner," because of her light brown complexion. Of Rudolph, Coach Temple said, "She's done more for her country that what the United States could pay her for."[14] Still, a greater amount of focus and attention on their feminine attributes than their athletic achievements and abilities remained the norm in the press for female athletes, and Wilma was no exception.

Historian Susan Cahn asserts that the accomplishments of Black women in sport in combination with the impact of the civil rights move-ment forced some changes in media policies in the early 1960s. As a result of such changes, African American women were photographed and featured more often in the press. Still, Cahn views the press coverage of

Wilma Rudolph as an exception to the rule. In a *Time* magazine feature, the news weekly declared "In a field of female endeavor in which the greatest stars have often been characterized by overdeveloped muscles and underdeveloped glands, Wilma (Skeeter) Rudolph has long, lissome legs and a pert charm."[15] According to Cahn, the newspaper coverage viewed women track athletes, who were predominantly Black, as "masculine freaks of nature." The coverage of Wilma was "the (feminine) exception." So, even as the newspapers applauded Wilma's charm and speed, the journalists and the press "resorted to stereotypical images of jungle animals," giving Wilma the nickname, "black gazelle." So, despite her feminine portrayal, the newspapers still viewed her in similar ways as her African American teammates, and "she was represented as a wild beast, albeit a gentle, attractive creature who could be adopted as a pet of the American public."[16] Amy Bass indicates that, regardless of the intention, the nickname "gazelle" served to reinforce the "inference that black athletic ability is as natural as that of a delicate African deer."[17]

After the Games, Wilma and her teammates went on a whirlwind tour of European track meets that delayed their return trip home to the United States. The American team competed in track meets in Athens, Greece; London, England; Amsterdam, Holland; and throughout Germany in Cologne, Wuppertal, Frankfurt, and Berlin. The American team was invited to the Vatican to meet Pope John XXIII. Even though Wilma was a Baptist, she knew that it was an important occasion to meet the head of the Roman Catholic church. The Pope told the group that they were all winners and blessed the team. Coach Temple took Wilma and some of her teammates to London for the British Empire Games. It was rainy, cold, and everything Wilma had thought London would be. She was entered in the 100-meter dash and the 4x100-meter relay and won both.

Wilma remembers that she never lost another race that year in college and AAU competitions, and as a result, the animosity that had started in Rome among her American teammates was growing, even among her Tigerbelle teammates. She says that her Olympic roommate Lucinda Williams stuck with her "like a true sister," but some of her teammates even stopped talking to her. One night, after running in the rain at one of the European competitions, her teammates hid the hot curlers so that Wilma was forced to attend that evening's banquet with messed up hair. Of course, this was a violation of Coach Temple's rules about cleaning yourself up after a race and presenting yourself like a lady in public. Perhaps that was part of her jealous teammates' plan. When Wilma showed up to the banquet with wet hair, Coach Temple was very upset and called a meeting with the team. No one owned up to the slight.

Wilma and her three Olympic teammates were set to run the 4x100 relay in the British Empire Games. Relays rely on every person to give their best and the success of a relay is about four runners making it around the track, not one person running the entire race. In this case, it might have been better had Wilma run it on her own. She recalls that her three teammates "decided they just weren't going to run that day, that they'd go out there and run maybe just as fast as it took for them to stay in the race, no faster."[18] Their strategy worked and by the time Wilma got the baton, she was well behind the leading team. She poured it on and ran the fastest anchor leg of her life, catching up to the leader and winning the race. Coach Temple told the other three girls that when they returned to Tennessee State they would all be on probation for their actions. This did not help the tense situation with Wilma and her teammates and there was still more running to do before heading back to the States. After traveling in Europe for three weeks, the team was finally heading home. The tension among the teammates was high, and everyone was more than ready to get back to Tennessee and the United States.

Wilma and her teammates were greeted at the Nashville airport by television stations, governor Buford Ellington, the mayor of Nashville, and a large crowd of friends, family, and fellow TSU students. Coach Temple told Wilma that she had to stay in Nashville for a couple of more days before heading home to Clarksville because the town was planning something special for her and needed a little more time to prepare. Wilma couldn't wait and that night, she found someone who would bring her home to see her parents and have her back in the dorms by the morning.

The town of Clarksville prepared a huge parade for Wilma to honor her Olympic accomplishments. At the time, in 1960, Clarksville was still a segregated city of 40,000 people. She had told the governor that she would not participate in a parade unless the event was integrated and as a result, Wilma's victory parade was the first integrated event held in her hometown of Clarksville. The parade started two miles out of town and had a police escort. Her parents, one of her brothers and his wife, and baby Yolanda were also in a car in the motorcade. The people of Clarksville, Black and White alike, lined the streets to welcome home their hometown heroine, Wilma Rudolph. Traditional all-White organizations, such as the American Legion, the Elks, and the VFW, participated in the parade. The traditional Black organizations were also marching in the parade, including the Burt High School

marching band, Black ministers, and other Black fraternal organizations. The mayor himself led the parade. The only person missing was
Robert Eldridge, Wilma's former boyfriend, who was visiting relatives
in Indiana.

The celebration banquet that night was also integrated, another first
for Clarksville; 1,100 Black and White people eating dinner together.
The significance was not lost on the group. Judge Hudson, who was
White, spoke metaphorically about the importance when he said, "Ladies
and gentleman, you play a piano. You can play very nice music on a piano
by playing only the black keys on it, and you can play very nice music
on the same piano by playing only the white keys on it. But, ladies and
gentleman, the absolute best music comes out of that piano when you
play both the black keys and the white keys together."[19] For the next few
days, Wilma was so busy meeting with people in Clarksville and talking
to reporters, that she hardly saw her family.

After the Clarksville celebration, Wilma headed to Chicago where
she was greeted by Mayor Richard Daley and received the key to
the city. Then it was off to a banquet in Detroit. Most of these events
were planned by the Tennessee State alumni association, and Wilma was
usually accompanied by her mother and Coach Temple. She went to an
event in Atlanta, met the NAACP in New York City, was presented at a
cotillion ball in Philadelphia, and met ambassadors in Washington, D.C.
She even appeared on the "Ed Sullivan Show," one of the most popular
television shows at the time. She made over 100 appearances in the
months after her Olympic triumphs.

Wilma received numerous awards and recognition over the next several months. For her Olympic accomplishments, she was awarded the
Associated Press Female Athlete of the Year in 1960, becoming only
the second African American woman to win the award (tennis player
Althea Gibson had been the first). She finished second in the voting
to Olympic teammate Rafer Johnson for the James E. Sullivan Award,
given to the top American amateur athlete. She was the first American
to win Italy's Christopher Columbus award, which was given each year to
the most outstanding international sports personality. She was awarded
the 1960 Helms World Trophy for North America, which was created by
Paul W. Helms and awarded to honor the best athlete on each continent.
She received the Los Angeles Times Award for women's track and field.
She was voted the most outstanding athlete of the year by the European
Sportswriters Association. Mademoiselle, the fashion magazine, selected
her to receive 1 of their 10 awards for outstanding achievements; she
was chosen as 1 of the 10 most outstanding women in the United States

by the *New York Times*; she received the Sports Magazine Award for top performer in track and field and the Betty Crocker Award for outstanding achievement; and she was selected by the *Nashville Banner* as its outstanding athlete. Wilma received the National Newspaper Publishers Association's Russwurm Award and was awarded the Babe Didrikson Zaharias Award in 1960 as the outstanding female athlete in the United States. She received a personal citation from the governor of Tennessee for outstanding achievement in 1960.[20] She met famous Black celebrities, like singers Lena Horne and Harry Belafonte. There was no end to the accolades for her stellar Olympic performance.

After the whirlwind tour of post-Olympic track meets through Europe, the Clarksville parade, and all the events celebrating her victories, Wilma still had her studies at Tennessee State to concentrate on, as well as the upcoming track season to prepare for. She hardly attended school that year, but when she did, she worked for Coach Temple at the post office making $62 a week. She pledged a sorority, Delta Sigma Theta, and life was getting back to normal, even with some of her teammates. She was not finished as a college runner just yet. In fact, she had two seasons left to compete as one of Temple's Tigerbelles and a track circuit that was calling her name.

NOTES

1. Althea Gibson, *I Always Wanted to Be Somebody*, (New York: Harper Collins, 1958), 33.

2. South Africa was readmitted to the Olympic Games in 1992.

3. Of the 25 American women on the U.S. Olympic Track and Field team, 15 were African American, with 7 Tigerbelles.

4. Wilma Rudolph, with Martin Ralbovsky, *Wilma: The Story of Wilma Rudolph* (New York: Signet, 1977), 128.

5. "The Fastest Female," *Time*, 19 September 1960, 74–75.

6. Dwight Lewis and Susan Thomas, *A Will to Win* (Mt. Juliet, TN: Cumberland Press, 1983), 138.

7. "The Fastest Female," *Time*, 19 September 1960, 74–75.

8. Jesse Owens had won four gold medals at the 1936 Olympic Games in Berlin, Germany. His four gold medals were in the 100-meter and 200-meter races, 4x100-meter relay, and the long jump.

9. Lewis and Thomas, *A Will to Win*, 134.

10. For more on Earlene Brown, see Michael D. Davis, *Black American Women in Olympic Track and Field* (Jefferson, NC: McFarland & Company, 1992), 23–37.

11. Davis, *Black American Women*, 33.

12. Allison Danzig, "Norton Runs out of Passing Zone," *New York Times*, 9 September 1960, 20.

13. Robert M. Lipsyte, "Wilma Rudolph Pauses Briefly for Medal, Visit and Plaudits," *New York Times*, 27 September 1960, 46.

14. Barbara Heilman, "Like Nothing Else in Tennessee," *Sports Illustrated*, 14 November 1960, 50; Scorecard, *Sports Illustrated*, 13 February 1961.

15. Susan Cahn, *Coming on Strong: Gender and Sexuality in Twentieth-Century Women's Sport* (New York: The Free Press, 1994), 137; "The Fastest Female," *Time*, 19 September 1960, 74.

16. Cahn, *Coming on Strong*, 137.

17. Amy Bass, *Not the Triumph but the Struggle: The 1968 Olympics and the Making of the Black Athlete* (Minneapolis: University of Minnesota, 2002), 404.

18. Rudolph, *Wilma*, 139.

19. Rudolph, *Wilma*, 145.

20. A. S. "Doc" Young, *Negro Firsts in Sports* (Chicago: Johnson Publishing Company, 1963), 269.

Chapter 8

WILMA'S POST-OLYMPIC COMPETITIONS

In addition to competing as a Tigerbelle, Wilma was also receiving invitations to run in several prominent track meets. The 1961 indoor track season was very exciting for Wilma. She was the first woman invited in several decades to run at the New York Athletic Club, the Millrose Games, the Los Angeles Times Games, the Penn Relays, and the Drake Relays, all races typically reserved for male athletes. Because Wilma was invited, it also opened competitions up for other female athletes. Due to the limited size of the indoor track, she would not run her best events, the 100-meter and 200-meter races, but instead had to run shorter distances, like the 50-, 60-, and 70-yard races. She did not win every race, sometimes having trouble with the shorter distances, and she felt tremendous pressure on her to repeat her Olympic feats. Wilma admitted that she didn't really enjoy running indoor races and that she felt like an "Amazon in an arena, performing for the blood-thirsty crowds."[1] The pressure to win was tremendous. Wilma told close friends that "once you've won three gold medals in the Olympics, everybody thinks you should be able to beat everyone else, anywhere, anytime, any place."[2]

At the Los Angeles Invitational in January 1961, Rudolph continued to dominate the track and celebrity circuit as a personality, even if she wasn't always finishing in first place. Sports reporter Jim Murray wrote, "She made herself gracefully available for interviews, and Los Angeles welcomed her from city council to movie set.... Los Angeles fans stormed the sports arena in such numbers that a sellout was posted one hour before opening ceremonies, and the shutouts were offering $6 for $2 seats, with no takers. For the 13,622 who got inside, the show was well worth it. Wilma, who appeared to be having the time of her young life, showed up poised, friendly, innocently flirtatious and nine pounds heavier than she had been at Rome."[3] Track and field fans loved Wilma's speed and grace. "Wilma won without bothering to remove her wristwatch, and there was some indication she could have carried her purse. Everyone in the massive sports arena, possibly excepting the girls she defeated, was quite in love with Wilma Rudolph."[4] Murray, like other reporters at the time, always tended to include comments that focused on Wilma's feminine appearance, often comparing her to other female athletes who were not as attractive. Her beauty was seen as a bonus, although it sometimes seemed more important than her athletic accomplishments. *Newsweek* magazine commented that Wilma's appeal was twofold; "Unlike most American female sprinters, she wins; and, unlike many American female athletes, she looks feminine."[5]

Wilma was still technically an amateur athlete, as there were no opportunities to run professionally at this time. While travel expenses were covered for athletes, she did not earn a living at these track meets, and her only income came from her campus jobs.

In February 1961, she ran the 60-yard dash at the Millrose Games in Madison Square Garden in New York City, traditionally an all-male track meet. She won the event in a world record time of 6.9 seconds, after running 7.4 seconds in the preliminary heats, beating Vivian Brown and Barbara Brown. Newspaper coverage continued to focus on Rudolph as "the attractive sprinter," and her personal life; "Consequently there is little time for Wilma Rudolph the co-ed, whose primary interests are her studies in elementary education, stylish frocks, dancing and 'just plain female gossip.'" Some of the gossip *Newsweek* reported was that the romantic relationship that seemed to blossom between Wilma and Ray Norton at the Olympics was over. When asked about it, Wilma replied that Ray had recently gotten married and the two remained good friends.[6] She discussed the hesitancy of friends to approach her since her Olympic success and how much she missed the "easy camaraderie" she enjoyed on campus prior to the Games. Of her fame, she admitted, "A girl wants to be liked for herself, not just because she can run fast. That's why I go out only with fellows I've known long before all the fuss started." In the same article, she continues to emphasize her femininity when she admitted that as much as she likes basketball, she was not a tomboy, and pointed to her skirt as proof positive.[7] Coach Temple echoed that sentiment stating that "Skeeter never makes the common mistake of trying to prove she's as good as a man. She's a woman." Not only was she not a tomboy, but according to Coach Temple, she knew her place, and that meant not trying to be better than men. At the end of the race, another reporter noted that Wilma's first response was to ask for a mirror and a comb.[8] All of these comments and press coverage indicate the concern related to Wilma's (and any other female athletes') femininity.

The next night, Wilma set a new world record in the 70-yard dash in Louisville, Kentucky, at the Mason-Dixie Games running the race in 7.8 seconds. Two world records in 24 hours! Two weeks later, she was racing in New York again, this time at the traditionally all-male New York Athletic Club track meet. She bettered her world record in the 60-yard dash in a speedy 6.8 seconds. In March, the travel finally got to Wilma and she faltered at the AAU indoor championships. In the preliminary heats of the 200-yard dash, Wilma was on fire and seemed unbeatable, but in the finals she was beat by her roommate from Tennessee State, the freshman Vivian Brown. It was the first race Wilma had lost in a long time, and it would not be her only loss that evening. In the 440-yard relay, Tennessee State was favored to win as they had done the previous seven years, but the relay lost to a young foursome running for Mayor Daley's Youth Foundation from Chicago. Wilma had no time to rest as there were more track meets and more appearances.[9]

On April 14, 1961, during a trip to Washington, D.C., for a public appearance for the General Mills food company, Wilma was able to meet President John F. Kennedy and Vice President Lyndon Johnson. She visited with Vice President Johnson with her mother, Coach Temple, and Bobby Logan, a friend from Fort Worth, Texas, and fellow Tennessee State student, who had arranged the visit. Wilma was discussing physical fitness with Vice President Johnson when Johnson said he thought she should meet with the President. She was turned off by Vice President Johnson who had put his feet up on the desk while he talked with them, but her meeting with President Kennedy was something special. She was led into the Oval Office and discussed sports and the Olympics with the secret service officers while she waited for the President. When President Kennedy arrived, he went to sit in his rocking chair and completely missed the chair landing on the floor. Everyone was stunned and not sure how to respond until the President laughed and indicated it was alright for everyone else to laugh about the fall. He explained that he was nervous about meeting an Olympic champion. They talked for over 35 minutes about sports, the Olympics, the nicknames Italian newspapers had given her, and what an honor it was for him to meet an Olympian.[10]

In July 1961, Wilma competed in the 100-yard dash and the 440-yard relay at the AAU outdoor championships in Gary, Indiana. Winners from this meet would run for the U.S. team in Europe that summer. Wilma won the 100-yard dash AAU title in 1961 in 10.8 seconds, her third consecutive AAU title in the sprint. She completed her title reign winning the 100-yard dash in 1962 with the same time of 10.8 seconds. As a result of winning the 100-yard dash, Wilma was selected to participate on the U.S. team that would compete across Europe. The U.S. team was coached by Marian Armstrong-Perkins, and some of Wilma's teammates included Willye White, Vivian Brown, Jo Ann Terry, Edith McGuire, and Ernestine Pollard. The team competed all across Europe, including West Germany, Ireland, London, and Moscow. In Moscow, she equaled her world record time in the 100 meters and anchored the U.S. relay team to victory. On July 19, 1961, Wilma raced in Stuttgart, Germany, and set a new world record in the 100-meter dash in a blazing 11.2 seconds.

Wilma surprised many people when she got married on October 14, 1961, to William Ward of Linden, New Jersey, who was also a student and track athlete at Tennessee State. In her autobiography, she never mentions her marriage (or any sort of friendship) to Mr. Ward and even indicates that upon her return from Rome, she and Robert Eldridge had resumed dating.[11] The marriage to Ward did not last long, and she was divorced a year later.

Wilma closed out 1961 with more awards, winning the Associated Press Female Athlete of the Year award for the second year in a row, beating golfer Mickey Wright and tennis player Darlene Hard, becoming the first track and field athlete to win the award twice. Wilma had been listed first on 178 ballots and received twice the number of points as the runner-up (592 to 270 points).[12] She was also the 1961 winner of the coveted Sullivan Award as the top amateur athlete, male or female, in the United States, which she had finished second in voting the year before.

After her success at the 1960 Olympics and the whirlwind of meets the following year, Wilma began thinking about retiring from the sport. Because she had won three gold medals, the expectations for the 1964 Olympic Games would be to repeat with three more gold medals or she felt she would be considered a failure. That was tremendous pressure on Wilma, and even Coach Temple agreed that "To go back to the Olympics in 1964, and lose will diminish everything you've already accomplished."[13] Moreover, once she graduated and was no longer officially a Tigerbelle, training for the team would be much more difficult, as would travel to meets. She would have to bear the financial costs of training and traveling to meets, let alone the time commitment required to train for elite competition. Everything would have to come from Wilma, including the money, which she did not have.

Track and field in the 1960s was still firmly amateur, which meant that athletes representing the United States could not receive prize money for victories, and were not funded during their training. So any athlete no longer on an organized team, such as a college team, Police Athletic League team, or Mayor Daley's Chicago team, was at a great disadvantage. Other personal factors weighed on Wilma's decision. In her autobiography she explains that she was dating Robert again and even though her young daughter, Yolanda, was doing fine with her mother, Wilma had started to think about taking care of Yolanda and creating a family with Robert. However, this period of her life is a little unclear, because according to court records, Wilma was married to William Ward at the time. By the time she stopped racing in 1962, her marriage to Ward had ended in divorce and she was preparing to marry Robert, her high school sweetheart and the father of her child.

Wilma decided that she wanted to end her career on top. She would run some more races and finish with a bang. She wrote, "Go out running well, then end it. But don't end it until you're running well; if you're running poorly stay with it until you're back to where you belong, then leave. Give them something positive to remember you by."[14] After that decision, it was easy to keep running, and next on her list was a dual meet against the Russians. In 1962, Coach Temple had asked Wilma if she wanted to run against the Russians, she agreed, and continued to train. In fact, Coach Temple was training Wilma especially hard, and she suspected it was to keep her busy and away from Robert. Whatever their relationship, Coach Temple was not supportive of Wilma's involvement with Eldridge, as he distracted her from two things Temple thought more important, track and her college education. Coach Temple wanted her prepared to not only run against the Soviet Union, but to beat them. American women in track and field were steadily improving and showing signs of potential and promise, though they still were not expected to dominate track and field like their male counterparts. Tex Maule, a sports reporter for *Sports Illustrated*, wrote, "We will, of course, win the men's competition. We won't be disgraced in the women's."[15]

Wilma's final track appearance was at a meet hosted by Stanford University in Palo Alto, California, at the end of July. Wilma was slated to run the 100-meter race and the 4x100-meter relay. There was great fanfare for the matchup between the American and Soviet athletes. She won easily beating her Soviet competitors in the 100-meter race, and got more competition from them in the relay. In the relay showdown, Wilma got the baton as the Russians zoomed past her, but like some other races, Wilma kicked in the speed and caught the Russian anchor leg to win the race. She received a standing ovation and simultaneously realized that she had just run her last race. She signed autographs for an hour and then gave her track shoes away to a little boy who had asked for her autograph. She was amused at the irony—"I didn't hang up my spikes. I gave them away."[16] Maule, writing for *Sports Illustrated*, reflected that the meet "not only was the best track meet of the year, it also was the prettiest. Soviet women athletes have always seemed more attractive than Soviet women clerks or housewives, and now the Americans are catching up in this new respect as well as in the events on the field. But it is difficult to be beautiful under the strain of competition.... But in action or repose, red or red-white-and-blue, black or white, male or female, no one in Palo Alto could match the incomparable Wilma Rudolph Ward for effortless grace and poise."[17] In 1962, Wilma won the Babe Didrikson Zaharias Award, given to the outstanding athlete of the world.[18] She was also named to the 1962 All-American AAU women's track and field team for her outstanding performances in the 100-yard, 100-meter, 220-yard, and 200-meter performances during the year.[19]

Wilma made a few more final appearances as a track athlete. She competed in Oslo, Norway, in August 1962, winning the 100-meters in 11.6 seconds.[20] She also ran, and lost, at the 1963 *Los Angeles Times* Invitational Meet. In May 1963, she represented the U.S. State Department, like her teammate Mae Faggs had done years before, at the Games of Friendship, which was a track and field meet held in Dakar, Senegal. The trip to Africa seemed to leave an impression on Wilma, though she discusses it very briefly in her own accounts of her life. Wilbert C. Petty, a cultural affairs officer at the U.S. embassy in Dakar, wrote his own account of her African trip; "I do not know all of the various parts of the world that Wilma must have traveled since 1960, but I rather suspect that this was her first time in an area where black rather than white is the color that counts. She seemed delighted to be among 'the folks.' She was struck by the handsome beauty of the Sengalese people."[21] While on the trip to Africa, Wilma appeared on television and radio shows, met President Leopold Senghor of Senegal, and was questioned about race relations by students at the University of Dakar. She visited Accra, Ghana; Conakry, Guinea; Bamako, Mali; and Ouagadougou, Upper Volta.

When Wilma returned from her trip to Africa, she found out that her high school coach, Clinton Gray, had just been killed in an automobile accident.[22] She was extremely upset, but within days had to leave on another overseas trip, this time with American evangelist Billy Graham to Japan as a member of the Baptist Christian Athletes. That same month, on May 27, 1963, Wilma Rudolph graduated from Tennessee State with her college degree.[23] Only a few days after graduation, in an Associated Press photo, Wilma is photographed with leaders from the Black community in Clarksville trying to enter a locked segregated restaurant.[24] That summer, at the end of July, Wilma finally married Robert Eldridge, who she had been dating on and off since the seventh grade.

A. S. "Doc" Young, writing in 1963 and reinforcing her prerequisite femininity, noted that Wilma was the "first Negro woman athlete to draw worldwide praise for her beauty...and this is indisputable proof that 'things are getting better' for Negroes!"[25] He identified Wilma as a "Negro super star" in track and field, and included her on a list of other star athletes such as basketball players Wilt Chamberlain and Bill Russell, Willie Mays of baseball, and Jim Brown of football fame. She was the only woman on Young's list.[26] Not only had Wilma "captivated world attention and applause," she had "glamorized a sport" which had been "frowned upon by many Americans and she is the first Negro athlete to be generally praised as 'beautiful.' "[27] At the time, these were significant symbolic accomplishments.

Wilma was a significant presence in American track and field following her Olympic performances. Only a few years later, *Sports Illustrated* would identify Wilma and the Tennessee State Tigerbelle program as the main reason why American women's track and field was progressing. John Underwood wrote, "Total suspicion has not yet given way to total respect for American women who run on display; losing to Russian women is still accepted as a matter of course—no great disaster—though in deference to our own women we have quit calling the Russians 'muscle molls.' But there are continuing manifestations of progress and an expanding awareness of what women's track is all about. The President's national fitness program taking in as it did girls as well as boys, was a major boost....Tennessee State, a university with enlightened ideas about scholarships for women athletes, produced Wilma Rudolph, Edith McGuire and Wyomia Tyus and has an exemplary program under Ed Temple, the Olympic coach."[28] Wilma's running days were scarcely over, but her contributions to track and field were already being acknowledged. Despite her retirement from competition, Wilma was ready for life outside of sport. She had her college degree in hand, was married for the second time, and her five-year-old daughter, Yolanda, was living with her full time. The next big chapters in Wilma's life were just beginning.

NOTES

1. Wilma Rudolph, *Wilma: The Story of Wilma Rudolph* (New York: Signet, 1977), 147.

2. Dwight Lewis and Susan Thomas, *A Will to Win*, (Mt. Juliet, TN: Cumberland Press), 150.

3. James Murray, "A Big Night for Wilma," *Sports Illustrated*, 30 January 1961, 48.

4. Murray, "A Big Night for Wilma," 48–49.

5. "Girl on the Run," *Newsweek*, 6 February 1961, 54.

6. "Girl on the Run," *Newsweek*, 6 February 1961, 54.

7. Robert D. Teague, "Everyone has Wilma on the Run," *New York Times*, 4 February 1961, 11.

8. "Storming the Citadel," *Time*, 10 February 1961, 57.

9. Michael D. Davis, *Black American Women in Olympic Track and Field* (Jefferson, NC: McFarland & Company, 1992), 121–22.

10. "President is host to Wilma Rudolph," *New York Times*, 15 April 1961, 12.

11. "Wilma Rudolph Married," *New York Times*, 29 November 1961, 50; also see Robert J. Condon, *Great Women Athletes of the 20th Century* (Jefferson, NC: McFarland, 1991), 148.

12. "Wilma Rudolph Repeats as Top Female Athlete," *New York Times*, 19 December 1961, 45.

13. Rudolph, *Wilma*, 151.

14. Rudolph, *Wilma*, 151.

15. Tex Maule, "U.S. and U.S.S.R. About-Face," *Sports Illustrated*, 16 July 1962, 18–19, 54.

16. Rudolph, *Wilma*, 153.

17. Tex Maule, "Whirling Success for the U.S.," *Sports Illustrated*, 30 July 1962, 14.

18. Joan Ryan, *Contributions of Women: Sports* (Minneapolis, MN: Dillon Press, 1975), 61.

19. "Miss Rudolph heads Track team for '62," *New York Times*, 13 December 1962, 14.

20. "Mrs. Ward Captures Dash," *New York Times*, 29 August 1962, 43.

21. Davis, *Black American Women*, 126–27.

22. "Miss Rudolph's Coach Dies," *New York Times*, 10 April 1963, 22.

23. "Wilma Rudolph Graduates," *New York Times*, 28 May 1963, 61.

24. Tom Biracree, *Wilma Rudolph: Champion Athlete* (New York: Chelsea House Publishers, 1988), 95. Also see "Athlete in Protest," *New York Times*, 30 May 1963, 32; the article states that Wilma Rudolph was one of 300 African Americans attempting to get served at a drive-in restaurant in Clarksville.

25. A. S. "Doc" Young, *Negro Firsts in Sports* (Chicago: Johnson Publishing Company, 1963), 197.

26. Young, *Negro Firsts*, 265. He lists Wilma's married name as Ward.

27. Young, *Negro Firsts*, 268.

28. John Underwood, "This is the Way the Girls Go," *Sports Illustrated*, 10 May 1965, 45.

Chapter 9

WILMA RUDOLPH: AN AMERICAN IMAGE

What emerged, though, from the early phase of the movement in the late 1940s and 1950s was a sense that black Americans—well-represented by black athletes such as Jackie Robinson in the national pastime, as well as Althea Gibson and Wilma Rudolph in international competition—also contributed to America's democratic experiment. The black women who won at Wimbledon or held aloft their Olympic gold medals not only displayed individual athletic talents and embodied the aspirations of many other African Americans; they stood for the nation at large. Such, at least, was the ideal.[1]

—David Wiggins and Patrick Miller

Wilma Rudolph's victories at the 1960 Olympic Games were significant for reason that extended beyond the boundaries of the sporting arena. Her victories in sport represented the ideals of America—ideals that celebrated the accomplishments of African American women in a democratic nation. Their successes reinforced the principle of meritocracy; namely that if you work hard, you'll be successful, regardless of your skin color or economic standing. The Cold War between the United States and the Soviet Union was still a political reality and the two nations increasingly sought ways to prove the superiority of their societies. Wilma's victories in track and field became part of the broader American campaign focused on defeating the communist threat around the world.

Wilma's success in track and field also occurred at a time when there was an increasing amount of racial tension and civil rights activities in the United States. Despite the 1954 Brown versus the Board of Education Supreme Court ruling that had mandated the integration of the countries public school systems, the process of desegregation promised to be slow and challenging. A year after the court ruling, Emmett Till, an African American teenager visiting relatives in Mississippi, was murdered for allegedly flirting with a White woman. Later that year, Rosa Parks was jailed for her refusal to give up her seat to a White man, sparking the famous Montgomery bus boycott of 1956 and 1957 and providing future activists with new methods of fighting for racial equality. The federal government called in the military to facilitate the integration of Central High School in Little Rock, Arkansas, in 1957. In February 1960, only seven months before Wilma's gold medal performances, four students in Greensboro, North Carolina, sat at a Whites-only counter at Woolworth's (a department store) and demanded service and refused to move until they were served; setting off the sit-in movement. The Reverend Martin Luther King, Jr., was at the forefront of the civil rights movement during this time period and led boycotts and marches fighting for the civil rights of Black Americans. The Soviet Union capitalized on the racial strife in America and skillfully used the images of violence against African Americans as evidence that democracy was only applicable for some Americans. The Soviets challenged American claims of equality and justice by pointing out the blatant inequities that existed between White and Black Americans, which contributed to an acceleration of the U.S. campaign to spread their version of democracy around the globe.

As part of the American government's campaign to educate the rest of the world community about American democracy and to promote images of harmonious race relations, the U.S. Information Agency (USIA) produced and distributed documentary films to nations around the world, translated in over 40 languages, highlighting the successes of African American celebrities as symbols of racial progress. Between 1953 and 1961, the USIA spent millions of dollars "to explain US foreign policy and to present the best face of American culture to the rest of the world."[2] The USIA was a consolidation of the government overseas information programs, which served to explain American foreign policy to other nations. In the 1950s, largely as a result of colonialists losing their power and control, new nations were established in Asia, Africa, and Latin America. Both the United States and the Soviet Union engaged in an effort to promote their systems, capitalism and communism respectively, in these establishing countries. The USIA provided materials, such as pamphlets, articles, and films that served to present the best images of American life. The production of the documentaries on African American "stars" was part of the larger strategy to promote images of American democracy around the world while simultaneously serving to replace any negative television footage of American race relations, such as the military presence at Central High School as it desegregated, protest marches, and other civil demonstrations that often resulted in violence. Schwenk examines the USIA series on "Negro Stars" as part of an American propaganda campaign that celebrated the achievement of individual Black Americans while ignoring the racial problems encountered along the way to their successes.

Schwenk describes three presentational strategies employed in the USIA films. First, the subject of the film "was shown demonstrating his or her talent or achievement," such as singing, acting, or competing in an athletic contest. Second, the film provided "narrative information [which] linked the star to an American society ready and willing to embrace the qualities exhibited" by the film's subject; qualities like hard work, overcoming obstacles, and perseverance. Lastly, each film "demonstrated the material benefits of American democracy through images of the star's social and economic conditions" by showing the audience the individual in their home, school, or community. Schwenk asserts that the USIA films often presented an inaccurate portrait of the subject and American democracy.[3] African Americans highlighted in the "Negro Stars" series included singer Marian Anderson (film produced in 1952), Ralph Bunche, the Nobel Peace Prize winner in 1950 (1955), tennis player and Wimbledon champion Althea Gibson (1957), decathlete and Olympic gold medalist Rafer Johnson (1960), and three time Olympic gold medalist Wilma Rudolph (1961).

Wilma's documentary was titled "Wilma Rudolph: Olympic Champion." Following the pattern identified by Schwenk, where the subject demonstrates her skills, the video begins with images of Wilma sprinting to victory in a race at an indoor track competition. The narrator introduces the audience to the runner, "This is Wilma Rudolph, a 20-year-old American university student and track star...She has set several new world records."[4] The film then shifts to her Olympic exploits. With clips of unnamed athletes from around the world competing in a variety of sports, the narrator provides the setting for Wilma's athletic triple crown. "In the summer of 1960, the Olympic Games of Rome saw athletes of 85 countries taking part in the world's biggest sports festival. On the U.S. team was Wilma Rudolph. Rome staged the 17th Olympiad of modern times. 6000 athletes competed in 18 different sports."[5] With images of Wilma running all three races, the narration takes the viewer from race to race, gold medal to gold medal, all the way to the victory stand and some coverage of the closing ceremonies.

The scenery changes and the viewer looks at an aerial view of the city of Nashville, Tennessee, and Tennessee Agricultural and Industrial University, "the university Wilma currently attends with aspirations to become an elementary school teacher" and where she is a good student. This is consistent with Schwenk's second identified pattern, celebrating Wilma's qualities of being studious and liked by her peers. The documentary shows an image of Wilma's dormitory and tells the audience that at a university of nearly 3,500 students, "Wilma is very popular with her classmates."[6] The audience then sees Wilma attend a class taught by Ed Temple, who is also the coach of Wilma's track team. Wilma is then shown being welcomed into the home of the university's president, Dr. Walter Davis, who was a former athlete himself. His walls are adorned with trophies and newspaper clippings won by Wilma, her teammates, and other Tennessee State athletes. The audience is reminded that Wilma is carrying on a tradition at the school of combining scholarship with athletics.

Wilma is shown at track practice, stretching and warming up with her Tigerbelle teammates. The narrator reminds the audience that Wilma is part of a team effort and that her successes are partially a result of being a member of the team. He narrates, "Wilma trains every day with her teammates. She is a true champion. And despite her youth, something of a veteran. She was at the Melbourne Olympics in 1956 with Coach Ed Temple's team. It's hard to believe now, but Wilma did not learn to walk until she was seven. She had to overcome a childhood disease. Ed Temple is proud of her, but he is proud of all his girls. After all, it took four of them to win the 400-meter relay at the Olympics."[7] Wilma is shown working at the university union post office, where she is able to meet other classmates as well as receive her own personal fan, which comes from admirers and friends from all over the world. She has a social life as well, and is seen attending a basketball game with fellow Olympian and classmate long jumper Ralph Boston. The narrator remembers that Wilma used to be a great basketball player before her success in track and field.

Schwenk's third pattern is the visual demonstration of American democracy by showing the subject's social and economic conditions. The film does this throughout by filming Wilma competing in packed arenas, in her college classroom, and her job at the post office. To reinforce this theme, the film also includes footage from Wilma's family home and church. The documentary then travels to Clarksville, Tennessee, where Wilma grew up and where her family still resides. The audience sees footage of Wilma's welcome home celebration and parade, the only footage that includes Wilma interacting with White people. The narrator is heard, as the footage of the parade and visit home flash on the screen; "'Clarksville Welcomes You,' that sign and the acclaim of the mayor and city officials of her hometown greeted Wilma Rudolph on her return from the Olympics. The city fathers of Clarksville, the neighbors and townspeople, the superintendent of her school, all came to greet their heroine. And of course there was her family. Her mother and father, and brother; they rode together in the welcome home parade. This is Wilma's home where her family lives. When she came back from the Olympics, she showed them medals she had won. Her mother placed one of them around her neck. They talked about the Olympics, the young people she had met, the many friends she had made. Her sister Charlene is a promising athlete, her brother, her family, all are interested in sports and very proud of Wilma, not only the honors that have come her way, but of her as a person."[8] Wilma is seen walking up the church entrance holding the hand of a small girl identified as her little niece. The narrator tells the audience that being home and at church services, Wilma "feels close to her family and her friends and neighbors. She has been all over the world and made friends everywhere, but still there is no place like home surrounded by the people she has since childhood."[9]

In the final minutes of the 10-minute film, we see images of Wilma sitting with President John F. Kennedy and Vice-President Lyndon Johnson at the White House. Kennedy had "wanted to thank Wilma for the high example she has set for the nation's youth." The film returns where it began, with Wilma Rudolph running before the crowds in a crowded indoor track arena. As clips of her running and winning cross the screen, the narrator concludes with this closing, "All during the track season sport arenas all over the United States invite Wilma to take part in one contest after another. Like a true champion she accepts, laces her shoes, and always tries to do her best, keeping with her own standards of excellence. She keeps making sports history. She was voted woman athlete of the year 1960. They know her everywhere in the United States as a champion, as Wilma Rudolph, the girl with the winning smile."[10] The final shot is an image of a smiling Wilma.

Looking at this film over 40 years later, it is interesting and revealing to watch Wilma Rudolph's life sanitized for global consumption as part of an American strategy to deflect charges of racism. In many ways, it may have helped to convince Americans and other countries that racism did not prevent a young Black girl from becoming the fastest woman in the world. Schwenk contends that as the USIA produced the series over the decade, the films became increasingly "more intimate and detailed."[11] Directed by Walter de Hoog, an employee of the Hearst Newsreel Service, the Wilma film was an example of the new approach. de Hoog enjoyed the freedom of working with the USIA, who provided little oversight in the production of the film, with the implicit understanding that nothing negative be mentioned about American society. He had also directed the USIA film on tennis player Althea Gibson four years earlier.

Schwenk's criticism of de Hoog's version of Wilma's life begins with the reference to Wilma's childhood. While he briefly mentions that Wilma suffered a childhood illness, Schwenk notes that he does not reveal her to be the 20th of 22 children born into a family living in poverty. Unlike some of the previous USIA films that included images of the "Negro star" being accepted by White America, de Hoog emphasized how Wilma flourished in an all Black setting at Tennessee State, without ever acknowledging that the college was all Black. Schwenk indicates that the film fails to explain that Tennessee State is a historically Black college and the role of these colleges in the American South. She contends that showing Wilma doing well at school was nothing unusual since "piety and love of learning were virtues USIA films were always happy to point out." What was out of the ordinary was for the films to show "African-Americans thriving socially and academically outside of white America."[12] Schwenk considers the footage of Wilma's Olympic victories to be the heart of the film suggesting that the "visual evidence of physical excellence, power and grace appears to stand as a 'seal of approval' for American democracy."[13] In her analysis, Schwenk explains that de Hoog was following USIA policy of "governmental silence" on race relations when he included footage of Wilma's welcome home celebration without mentioning that it was the first integrated celebration in the segregated town. Images of successful young African Americans in sports served as powerful visual evidence against the images seen regularly in television news footage of young African American college students who were physically assaulted as they fought to integrate schools, buses, and lunch counters.

One other important issue worth noting in the documentary version of Wilma's short life is the clip of Wilma walking up the church stairs holding the hand of her little niece. It seems highly plausible that the young girl was in fact Wilma's daughter, Yolanda, who would have been between two and three years old at the time of the filming. While friends and family would have known about Wilma's pregnancy, there is very little evidence to suggest that her teenage pregnancy was common knowledge in the sports world. That the USIA would try to pass Wilma's daughter off as her niece is consistent with the government's effort to present an image of her life as an American success story. Perhaps it was her desire as well. In October of 1961, the same year the USIA film was released, Wilma married fellow Tennessee State student William Ward, though there is no mention of her even having a boyfriend. The film does show a clip of Wilma attending a basketball game with classmate and fellow Olympian Ralph Boston, but there are no implications of a romance between the two star athletes.

In her autobiography, written over a decade after the filming of the documentary, Wilma curiously did not mention her participation in the filming of the documentary or her reaction to the film once it was released. Certainly it must have been noticeable to have film cameras with her in class, at her job, and in her family's living room. Nor does she remember her participation in the American campaign to promote racial harmony around the globe. In fact, despite her many victories over Soviet athletes, and athletes from other communist nations, Wilma never reflected on the Cold War politics impact on sport, nor her own victories over her communist opponents. During the time period that the film was produced, Wilma was still attending college and competing in track meets around the country. She was not finished with her athletic exploits, though she had begun thinking about her retirement from the sport. She wanted to retire a winner and to be remembered as a three-time Olympic gold medalist. Retirement from the athletic spotlight would prove to be challenging in more ways than one.

NOTES

1. David K. Wiggins and Patrick B. Miller, *The Unlevel Playing Field: A Documentary History of the African American Experience in Sport* (Urbana: University of Illinois Press, 2003).

2. Melinda M. Schwenk, "'Negro Stars' and the USIA's Portrait of Democracy," [Electronic version], *Race, Gender & Class* 8(4) (2001): 2, http://proquest.umi.com/pqdweb?index=0&did-494618441&SrchMode=1&sid=1&Fmt=3&VInst=PROD&VType=PQD&RQT=309&VName=PQD&TS=1135114541&clientId=17934 (accessed December 20, 2005).

3. Schwenk, "'Negro Stars,'" 1, 4, 5.

4. *Wilma Rudolph: Olympic Champion* [film] (1961). U.S. Information Agency. Available from Archives II, Record Group 306.5247.

5. *Wilma Rudolph: Olympic Champion* [film].
6. *Wilma Rudolph: Olympic Champion* [film].
7. *Wilma Rudolph: Olympic Champion* [film].
8. *Wilma Rudolph: Olympic Champion* [film].
9. *Wilma Rudolph: Olympic Champion* [film].
10. *Wilma Rudolph: Olympic Champion* [film].
11. Schwenk, "'Negro Stars,'" 8.
12. Schwenk, "'Negro Stars,'" 9.
13. Schwenk, "'Negro Stars,'" 9.

Chapter 10

HANGING UP
THE SPIKES: WILMA
IN RETIREMENT

Wilma wanted to be remembered for all of her accomplishments in track and field, and she wanted to leave the sport as a winner. She decided not to wait for the 1964 Olympic Games, instead making the decision to retire and move on with her life. After deciding that she would no longer compete in track and field, Wilma, now married to her high school sweetheart, Robert Eldridge, was ready to be a full-time mother and wife. *Jet* magazine had taken pictures of the wedding, and it was quite a social event. The reception was held at the American Legion hall. The only person who did not show up was Coach Temple, which hurt Wilma's feelings. She assumed it was because Coach Temple did not approve of her marriage to Robert. The young Mr. and Mrs. Eldridge could not afford a honeymoon, but celebrated their marriage by attending Robert's family reunion.

Robert decided that he wanted to attend college, and Wilma was determined to find a job to support the family and help put her husband through college. She found employment as a second grade teacher at Cobb Elementary School, the school she had attended as a young girl. She was also hired as the girls' track coach at her former high school, taking Coach Gray's old job. Wilma had been on one of her many trips receiving an honor when Coach Gray was killed, and she still had a difficult time dealing with his death. Wilma loved teaching second grade and felt the she was having a good influence on her students, but teaching at her old school was difficult. She had learned many new teaching methods during college, but her former teachers turned colleagues were set in their ways and not interested in new ways of teaching. This was very frustrating for Wilma. During her first year as a teacher, she became pregnant and at the end of the school year gave birth to her second daughter, Djuana.

That summer, Wilma watched the 1964 Olympic Games held in Tokyo, Japan, as she lay in bed with her new baby and was happy with where she was in life. She had no regrets about not running. She was featured in *Jet* magazine after the Tokyo Games, which updated readers on her whereabouts since her gold medal achievements four years prior. The magazine said she was married to Tennessee State basketball player, Robert Eldridge, and the couple recently welcomed a new addition, then four-month-old Djuana. There was no mention of daughter Yolanda. Wilma was 30 pounds heavier than she had been as an athlete, and was now focused on motherhood, which according to one photo caption was better than fame.[1] Wilma returned to teaching in the fall of 1964 and soon was pregnant again. In August 1965, Wilma gave birth to her third child, and first son, Robert, Jr. By this time, she had decided that she was ready to leave home and no longer wanted to stay in Tennessee. The family moved to Evansville, Indiana, where Wilma was hired as the director of a community center. However, this job was not what she expected, and she kept searching for the job she really wanted. Soon she was hired by the Job Corps Center in Poland Springs, Maine, to run the girls' physical education program, which involved writing the curriculum and leading the activities. She stayed in that position for almost a year.

In 1967, Wilma was invited to work for Vice President Hubert Humphrey as part of Operation Champ. Operation Champ took Olympic and professional athletes into the "16 largest city ghetto areas" to provide the youth in those areas with training in sports. Wilma traveled to Detroit, Cleveland, Chicago, Washington D.C., and Baltimore.[2] She and fellow Tennessee State grad and Olympian Ralph Boston taught track and field; Olympian Donna deVarona taught swimming; Ollie Matson, who had recently retired from the NFL's Philadelphia Eagles, taught football; and players from the NBA's Baltimore Bullets taught basketball. During this time period there were several riots in major American cities, including Detroit, Los Angeles, and Newark, and Wilma suspected that Operation Champ was designed to help calm things down and offer youth structured sporting activities to keep the youth out of trouble. Through Operation Champ, she saw the oppression of living in these areas firsthand and in some ways felt she understood better the emotions that had led to the rioting. Despite her upbringing in poverty and segregation, the urban settings were a new and stressful experience for Wilma.

After her brief stint with Operation Champ, Wilma asked the Job Corps to transfer her closer to home, and she moved her family to St. Louis, Missouri. The Job Corps Center was right in the middle of what Wilma called "the black ghetto area." However, she felt that she had just experienced that same type of environment with Operation Champ, and she was not prepared to deal with it so soon after. So Wilma and her family moved again, this time to Detroit, to help take care of her sister Charlene, who was ill. She was hired at Pelham Junior High School in Detroit and coached track. They stayed in Detroit for a year and a half until Wilma decided to move her family once again.

On the night Martin Luther King, Jr., was assassinated, April 4, 1968, Wilma's aunt had also died earlier that day in Clarksville. Wilma flew to Tennessee with her children and remembered the tensions she felt in the Nashville airport.[3] King's assassination stirred up many emotions and in the Nashville bus station, a White man spit on Wilma's children. The police arrested the man, but it was the end of a very bad day for the family. She mourned for her aunt and for Dr. King. Not sure of where to head next, she was encouraged to move to California by fellow 1956 Olympian Bill Russell, a basketball player for the Boston Celtics.[4] She lived in Los Angeles and worked for the Watts Community Action Committee. While she enjoyed the work, she did not make much money and had a hard time taking care of her family and making ends meet.

In March 1969, Wilma was invited to Italy by an Italian newspaper publisher who remembered her from the Olympics. The trip was free and she was in need of some relaxation. She admitted that she was searching for some peace of mind; "I had been a good mother and a good wife, but I was besieged with money problems; people were always expecting me to be a star, but I wasn't making the money to live like one. I felt exploited both as a woman and as a black person."[5] She caught a cold on the trip and stayed in bed recuperating. At one point it was rumored in *Paese Sera*, a communist newspaper, that she was being held prisoner. The article said that Wilma "was jobless and so poor that she had had to relinquish care of her three children and had had to pawn her Olympic trophies. The accounts also said that she had been denied employment in the United States because she is a Negro."[6]

In response to the articles, Wilma held a press conference and announced that she was fine and heading back home to the United States. According to Wilma's autobiography, the Italian publisher that had paid for her trip had wanted her to speak out against America and capitalism. However, according to the *New York Times*, Wilma had been brought to Rome by *Il Tempo*, the "right wing morning daily" in Rome, to refute the rumored stories. In *Il Tempo*, Wilma stated that she had not sold her medals and had no intention of selling them. She was living off her life savings after injuring herself in an automobile accident in November 1967.[7] She said she was temporarily unemployed because she wouldn't take a job for any salary lower than what she thought she was worth. According to the *New York Times*, Wilma was considering taking a research job with the Afro-American Cultural Center of the University of California, Los Angeles. When asked about mistreatment because of her skin color, "Miss Rudolph shook the heavy silver earrings that hung below her expansive frizzy coiffure and said: 'I can't think of one Negro who hasn't had trouble because of skin color.'"[8]

Wilma went on to discuss racial politics in America, expressing her support for Tommie Smith and John Carlos, two African American Olympians who had raised their black gloved fists in the air on the victory stand at the 1968 Games, and stating that she respected all Black leaders in the United States. She declared herself as "not non-violent," which she explained to mean that she wouldn't go out and "burn down 40 stores, but if somebody hit me, I certainly wouldn't turn the other cheek.'"[9] Such a pointed comment reveals how many of Wilma's more difficult experiences were not addressed in her autobiography. The comment was published in 1969, well before her 1977 book, but in her book she never expresses any thoughts related to the 1968 Olympic stand protest by Smith and Carlos, nor does she express any views related to the civil rights movement and the conflicting ideas different groups had related to the use of violence. It was also on this trip to Italy that Wilma visited with Pope Paul VI, who presented her with a medal commemorating his reign.[10]

Upon returning to California, Wilma was hired as an administrator in the Afro-American Studies program at UCLA. Like similar jobs, Wilma felt as if her co-workers were holding her track successes against her. Wilma reports that most of her co-workers doubted her skills for the job, and suspected that she was hired because of her success in athletics. It is unclear how long Wilma stayed at this job, and it is not discussed in much detail in her book.

In the fall of 1970, Wilma was hired at Sacramento State College (SSC) as the women's track and field instructor in the physical education department. She was friends with Stan Wright, the head coach of the SSC men's track team who had been an Olympic coach for the 1968 U.S. men's team. Wright was the California school's first African American coach. There was no women's track team, so Wilma assisted Coach Wright with the men's team. Wilma stayed less than a year in the position and was very unhappy during her time in Sacramento. She admitted to hating the job. "It wasn't a challenge," she said in an interview years later. "Later on in life I discovered that in order for me to be successful I had to have a challenge. I can't do a nine to five job. After I left my job at the college, I found myself going into different fields without knowing anything. It was difficult to find employment here. There were good jobs, but they were never what I wanted to do. Somehow, people always thought of Wilma Rudolph as a threat. In college I was an education major and qualified for several jobs. But the fame that came with the Olympic medals was too threatening to many people. Being a woman, being black and being Wilma Rudolph worked against me while I was living here. I tried to do all the right things, but it was difficult. I never tried to cash in on my medals, but things weren't working out well. All people could see was Wilma Rudolph the track runner."[11] She was very disappointed in the Sacramento State job and admitted to crying herself to sleep on occasion. She gave birth to her fourth child and second son, Xurry, in 1971.[12]

Wilma did not address specifics related to her numerous jobs in her autobiography, so interviews with her in her later years become important in trying to establish not only where she worked, but what sort of work conditions she encountered. She also fails to indicate what her husband Robert was doing for employment and if he accompanied the family on the various job relocations. She writes in general terms as it relates to her several jobs and the expectations she thought people had of her because she was a famous Olympian. Overall, in her autobiography, Wilma never dwells on her employment failures, and even fails to mention several of the many positions she held throughout the 1960s and 1970s. She recounted in an interview published in *Ebony*, "You become world famous and you sit with kings and queens, and then your first job is just a job. You can't go back to living the way you did before because you've been taken out of one setting and shown the other. That becomes a struggle and makes *you* struggle."[13]

For a brief time in the early 1970s, Wilma worked as a commentator on West German television before she started looking for another job and finally landed one with Mayor Daley's Youth Foundation program in Chicago in 1973. She was charged with establishing training sites for youth all over Chicago. This job presented her with the opportunity to get her oldest daughter, 12-year-old Yolanda, involved in running track. Of her daughter's interest in following her mother's footsteps Wilma said,

"She was late in beginning to run. I wanted her to be sure she wanted to run and I didn't try to motivate her to entering track early."[14] Five years later, Yolanda would enter Tennessee State on a partial scholarship to run track with Coach Temple and the Tigerbelles.[15]

Wilma's job with Mayor Daley's Youth Foundation was also short lived. Again, Wilma felt she was valued for her Olympic reputation and nothing else. Her next stop was in Charleston, West Virginia, to help raise funds for a Track and Field Hall of Fame. Of course Wilma was supportive of the project—track had been the arena of her greatest accomplishments. When the funds were finally raised, Wilma left West Virginia. She was in debt, Robert was ill, and she thought it best to head back home to Tennessee.

Sometime in the 1970s, though she does not discuss it in her book, Wilma decided to start her own business, Wilma Unlimited, designed to help underprivileged youth get involved in track and field. She was hired to appear in a Geritol magazine ad in 1976. She lectured on college campuses and wrote her autobiography in 1977, which was then turned into a NBC-TV movie starring Cicely Tyson as her mother. It was written, directed, and produced by Bud Greenspan, the noted Olympic film maker. The movie did not result in any additional opportunities for Wilma to make money from her Olympic experiences, but she did serve as a consultant to the film. She also served as a film production consultant to the Tennessee Department of Economic Development.

Wilma returned to Tennessee State in 1978 to help participate in ceremonies honoring Coach Temple and the new 400-meter all-weather-track that was named in honor of the successful coach. Of Temple's 32 Tigerbelle Olympians, 31 attended the April 8th ceremonies, which Tennessee Governor Ray Blanton also decreed as Edward S. Temple Day. Over a 20 year period, Temple's Tigerbelles had set 9 Olympic records, and won 11 gold medals, 5 silver, and 4 bronze.[16] By this time however, the women's track team was not finding the same success it had in the 1950s and 1960s. With the integration of colleges and universities, many African American students who might have attended Tennessee State instead chose schools that were predominantly White colleges. Moreover, with the increased attention given to women's sport program as a result of Title IX legislation, there was more funding for women's teams, also hurting Tennessee State's ability to recruit quality female athletes.

In 1980, Wilma officially ended her 17-year marriage to Robert, reasoning that she had grown and he had not. She explained that while her world had grown bigger, his had become smaller. He had wanted a housewife, and she had been one for a number of years. She admitted that the marriage "never worked."[17] She had recently started painting and sold her first painting for $10,000. She had a new attitude. "I love Wilma, and that's what makes me tick. I'm honest with myself, so everything sad that had happened in my life no longer matters. My motivation now is being free, being able to create, and being in a position to grow emotionally. If I was ever bitter, it was during those years when I was very young."[18] On December 2, 1980, Tennessee State University named its indoor track for Wilma Rudolph. In 1981, she started the Wilma Rudolph Foundation, a nonprofit organization, which was established to help train young athletes, and an extension of her Wilma Unlimited program. The foundation was located in Indianapolis, Indiana, and by the mid-1980s had over 1,000 participants who received free coaching. In 1983, Wilma was inducted into the Tennessee State University Hall of Fame.

In a "What Ever Happened to...?" feature on Wilma in *Ebony*, Wilma spoke of her personal life, telling the magazine that she was not currently dating anyone, and that she would definitely never get married again. She proclaimed, "I love being free. Maybe one day I'll find somebody and be serious about dating. But my social life right now is the pits. I like people to like me for me, not because I'm Wilma Rudolph."[19] The article indicated that Wilma was keeping herself busy with endorsements, television appearances (including her own local cable show), and promotional work for the upcoming Los Angeles Olympic Games. She was also active playing tennis, her new favorite athletic activity. In 1987, she returned to coaching to work as a track coach at DePauw University in Indiana. She loved working with young athletes.

At some point in the 1980s, Wilma experienced rough times, burdened by extended family members and their financial needs, having her house repossessed, and the federal government coming after her for taxes. There were rumors of Wilma being involved with drugs. Reporter Sam Lacy sees this as a time when Wilma was down morally. Admirably, just as she had many times before, Wilma recovered from these difficult times.[20]

Living back in Tennessee in the 1990s, Wilma became the vice-president of Nashville's Baptist Hospital in 1992. In 1993, Wilma was reunited with her 1960 Olympic teammate, boxer Muhammad Ali, at a White House event honoring the two athletes as "Great Ones." Only a year later, in July of 1994, Wilma was diagnosed with brain and throat cancer. Though she did not want people to see her sick, she would visit the Tennessee State campus and walk arm in arm with Coach Temple, now retired, around the track. She died on November 12, 1994, at her home in Brentwood, Tennessee, of a malignant brain tumor at the young age of 54. At the November 17 service at TSU's Kean Hall, thousands of people paid their respects at a memorial service. Her funeral was held at Clarksville's First Baptist Church and Tennessee flags flew at half-mast. Her casket was draped with the Olympic flag.

Life had not been easy since hanging up her track shoes, but throughout her adulthood, Wilma had been a devoted mother who valued her children more than anything. What the world had now was only memories of an incredible competitor and a woman who had achieved remarkably against all odds in track and field; her life, in reality, was much more difficult. Wilma stated that running in the Olympics, "sort of sent my way all the other positive things and feelings that I've ever had. That one accomplishment—what happened in 1960—nobody can take from me. It wasn't something somebody handed me."[21] That would be the legacy of Wilma Rudolph.

NOTES

1. "Unbeatable Wilma Sheds No Tears Over Track," *Jet* 5(November 1964): 57.

2. Wilma Rudolph, with Martin Ralbovsky, *Wilma: The Story of Wilma Rudolph*, (New York: Signet, 1977), 160.

3. Rudolph, *Wilma*, 161.

4. Rudolph, *Wilma*, 162.

5. Rudolph, *Wilma*, 163.

6. Alfred Friendly, Jr., "Wilma Rudolph Denies Selling Medals," *New York Times*, 26 March 1969, 54.

7. Wilma does not mention her car accident in her autobiography.

8. Friendly, Jr., "Wilma Rudolph Denies Selling Medals," 54.

9. Friendly, Jr., "Wilma Rudolph Denies Selling Medals," 54.

10. "Pope Honors Miss Rudolph," *New York Times*, 27 May 1969, 57.

11. Zenobia Jonell Gerald, "Rudolph's Free to Run a Winning Streak," *Sacramento Bee*, 2 June 1981, B4.

12. Wilma does not mention her fourth child in her autobiography, although she dedicates it to all four children and her husband. On the last page of the book, she talks about her two sons playing football, but never indicated when the second son was born. In Tom Biracree's book, *Wilma Rudolph: Champion Athlete* (New York: Chelsea House Publishers, 1988), 100, he says that she gave birth to Xurry in 1971 and returned to work when Xurry was old enough, including work as a commentator for West German television and radio. However, an article in the *Sacramento Union*, states that she had recently given birth to a child when she was hired at Sacramento State in the autumn of 1970.

13. Anne Janette Johnson, *Great Women in Sports* (Detroit: Visible Ink Press), 407.

14. "She Runs in Mother's Footsteps," *New York Times*, 8 April 1973, 259.

15. "Wilma Rudolph Lends Grace to Reunion," *New York Times*, 28 March 1976, 170.

16. "Tennessee State Honors Coach with a New Track," *New York Times*, 9 April 1978, S4.

17. Gerald, "Rudolph's Free to Run a Winning Streak," B4. In an article written about Wilma when she was hired at Sacramento State College, it indicates that she was in fact married to William Ward at the time of her employment. See "Ex-Olympian On SSC Staff," *Sacramento Union*, 1 October 1970, B1. Ward was in the construction business. In her autobiography, she never mentions the position at Sacramento State College or William Ward.

18. Gerald, "Rudolph's Free to Run a Winning Streak," B5.

19. "Whatever happened to ... Wilma Rudolph?" *Ebony* (February, 1984): 86.

20. References made to the difficulties experienced by Wilma during this time are found viewing ESPN's "Wilma Rudolph, Fifty Great Athletes, #41," which aired on April 2, 1999.

21. "Whatever happened to ... Wilma Rudolph?" *Ebony* (February, 1984): 88.

Chapter 11

WILMA ON WILMA— WRITING HER OWN STORY

For much of Wilma Rudolph's adult life, she had been the subject of much attention because of her athletic successes at the 1960 Olympic Games. Her victories on the track seemed to represent something about America—that talent and hard work resulted in opportunities and success and that skin color could not stop success. In many ways, her story of overcoming poverty and illness to become an Olympic champion was a story that resonated with all of America. It was a true success story. After retiring from competition, Wilma worked in several jobs, most of which were disappointing experiences. In 1977, she decided to tell her own story using her own voice. In collaboration with Martin Ralbovsky as the editorial assistant, Wilma authored her autobiography titled *Wilma*.[1]

Michael Oriard, in an essay on the "African-American sports autobiography," delineates what that phrase indicates. Oriard suggests that "On the face of it, the autobiography of a black athlete is simply an account of that individual's experiences in and out of sport, but each of the three terms in the phrase 'African-American sports autobiography' complicates this straightforward understanding. An *autobiography*, whether St. Augustine's, Benjamin Franklin's, or Maya Angelou's, is not the transparent record of a lived life but the consciously crafted self-presentation of an individual framed by certain social, economic, and political contexts and guided by any number of personal motives...The *sports* autobiography, in contrast, is a commercial product arising from and contributing to American celebrity culture, rarely written by the athlete alone but 'with' or 'as told to' a professional writer."[2]

Wilma's autobiography, written in 1977, was part of a larger movement of prominent Black athletes writing their life stories, and this group, including boxers Muhammad Ali and Floyd Patterson, football player Jim Brown, and basketball players Bill Russell and Wilt Chamberlain, is credited with establishing the genre of African American sports autobiographies. Oriard contends that these autobiographies adopted the same formula, very similar to the patterns used by the USIA documentaries identified by Melinda Schwenk. Each autobiography includes the following elements: "early poverty, strong parental influence (whether from one parent or two), escape through sport, usually with the guidance of black or white mentors, hard work, setbacks, and triumphs."[3] These elements combine to create a "pattern of the American success story ... its appeal to readers in its utter familiarity, as well as its reassurances that talent and hard work can defeat all obstacles, even racial ones."[4] Wilma's story is no exception.

Wilma's narrative follows the pattern described by Oriard, beginning with her family's poor background and her parents,' especially her mother's, devotion to helping her overcome polio and paralysis. She writes of significant mentors, Coach Clinton Gray and Coach Ed Temple, two men who helped push Wilma to her athletic successes. And despite all the obstacles of poverty, illness, and teenage pregnancy, Wilma emerged as the fastest woman in the world. Quite a story when one considers her early troubles walking with a brace. Moreover, the obstacles of racism and sexism were not enough to stop Wilma from succeeding, and her reluctance to discuss both in any detail in her book reveals her efforts to dictate how her story was to be told and retold.

In her autobiography, Wilma writes an account of her life that reveals an individual who chose to not reflect too deeply on the negative experiences, and instead focused on the successful details of her life. She completely excluded important events and often times did not recall them entirely as they occurred. For example, Wilma writes that she attended her first AAU track and field championship meet in the summer of 1956 in Philadelphia, Pennsylvania, where she was very successful, winning every race she entered, and went on to compete in the Olympic Trials. However, Wilma actually competed in her first AAU championship meet in the summer of 1955 in Ponca City, Oklahoma, but she did not win first place at this meet, which might explain why she chose to not include it in her book. Although she also mentions that when she lost at the Tuskegee Relays, she found great motivation to work harder for future competitions, so she is not entirely unwilling to acknowledge failure. There seems to be no rhyme or reason behind her decisions to include some wins and losses, but not others. One must also consider that girls high school track and field did not receive much press attention, so Wilma could not simply go through all her old clippings to jog her memory—there were not many clippings of such events.

Besides not being entirely accurate in her remembrances related to her track and field performances, Wilma does not share some important personal information. For example, despite newspaper and magazine accounts that linked Wilma with fellow Olympic teammate Ray Norton, she never mentioned Norton in her autobiography. Nor does she mention Olympic long jumper and Tennessee State student Ralph Boston, though she was also linked with him and appeared in the USIA video with Boston at a Tennessee State basketball game. She fails to mention her first marriage to fellow Tennessee State student, William Ward. Even though this marriage lasted less than one year, certainly it merits inclusion in the writing of her life story. And though Robert Eldridge is mentioned throughout her book, she never really discusses anything about him beyond having an interest in him, him fathering her children, and their marriage ceremony. She doesn't indicate his interests, if he played sports in college, or what types of jobs he held after his college education. Again, though, Wilma does provide some very personal information, such as her teenage pregnancy, which indicates that she is willing to share personal details that don't always frame her in the best light. In fact, the pregnancy of her first child does contribute to the story of her success, as she needed the support of her family and Coach Temple to be able to keep running after becoming a mother.

Wilma also made the decision to not share much information on her life post-track and field. While she mentions some of the different jobs she held, she does not reveal the troubles she had keeping steady employment. Perhaps Wilma felt that to discuss some of her disappointments would be to expose too much of herself, and she did not want to dwell on moments she had considered as failures. Equally worthy of consideration is the ability of an individual to reflect on their life as it is being lived. In many ways it is quite understandable why Wilma Rudolph would choose to narrate her life story as one that emphasized courage, success, and hope. It would have made for a much more enjoyable writing experience and she had, in fact, accomplished some very remarkable achievements. Cindy Himes Gissendanner suggests that Wilma, through her personality and athletic excellence, rather than any type of political consciousness, was able to break down racial animosity in her hometown of Clarksville. She contends that Wilma's narrative served a purpose, both in supporting Wilma's personal triumphs, but also through the political and symbolic implications of her victories.[5] In a 1984 interview, Wilma proclaimed "No one has a life where everything that happened was good. I think the thing that made life good for me is that I never looked back. I've always been positive no matter what happened."[6]

Wilma's decision to tell her story as a positive, uplifting journey was similar to a decision to do the same made by another track and field female great, Babe Didrikson, perhaps revealing the challenge that athletic women were faced with prior to America's general acceptance and celebration of female athletes. Didrikson had competed for the United States in the 1932 Los Angeles Olympic Games and later became a founder of the Ladies Professional Golf Association. In her autobiography, *This Life I've Led: My Autobiography*, Didrikson chose to focus on certain aspects of her life that emphasized the positives—a conscious decision she made to help control her image and the public consumption of her image.[7] She never mentions the rumors that dogged her related to her sexuality, though it would later be revealed in a biography about her life that she had in fact been in a lesbian relationship, in spite of her marriage to wrestler and promoter George Zaharias. The stories are then perpetuated when another biography of Didrikson simply retells the stories the athlete had included in her own book and a made for television movie uses the two books to present an acceptable film version of Didrikson's life. Didrikson biographer Susan Cayleff addresses the discrepancies in Didrikson's autobiographical accounts, and her investigation revealed a much different woman than originally presented by Babe herself. Despite such discrepancies, Babe Didrikson was a tremendous athlete. So why did her narrative exclude a major relationship in her life? Earlier newspaper accounts of Didrikson's athletic exploits routinely critiqued her femininity or lack of and included disparaging remarks about her unattractiveness. She had been dogged by the press and labeled with mannish stereotypes, marrying Zaharias, changing her clothing and hair style, and switching to a career in a more appropriate sport, golf, were part of a strategy to restore her image. Her autobiography, now read with the knowledge of the Cayleff biography, presents compelling evidence of how powerful gender expectations were in the first half of the twentieth century.

Cayleff's findings can be instrumental in our reading of Wilma Rudolph and her presentation of her life experiences. One must assume that Wilma had to deal with racism and sexism which undoubtedly influenced her and what she was able to do and not do, simply because of the time period in which she lived. Still, Wilma makes little reference to racism in her book, and writes almost nothing on sexism and what it was like to compete as a female in a male dominated arena. One must certainly consider the times in which she was writing and the audience she hoped to reach. She is never clear about who she thinks might be reading her book, though it would have been appealing to both young female athletes and Americans wanting to be reminded of another American success, rags to riches story of meritocracy. One must also bear in mind that her image was built solidly on a narrative about triumph, about overcoming odds, and ultimately about coming out on top. To address racism and sexism, or to even include incidents where she was not able to emerge victorious, simply would not have been consistent with the public persona of Wilma Rudolph. Even though newspaper interviews reveal some of her frustrations, her own recollections do not include such personal thoughts. To have dwelled on her shortcomings and failures would have gone against the narrative devised for Black athletes during this time period of the 1960s and 1970s. Oriard contends that autobiographies were designed to present a "pattern of the American success story" which would be appealing to a readership that wanted "reassurances that talent and hard work can defeat all obstacles, even racial ones."[8] This meant that Wilma's written account of her life would require the omission of several important moments that would force the readers, and Wilma herself, to acknowledge the impact that structural racism had and continues to have on African Americans, as well as the influence of sexism in American society. Who wants to read a story of how a crippled girl learned to run faster than anyone else, but that after she won her races, she was not able to capitalize on her successes because employers did not want to hire her based on her skin color and her gender? Maybe in 1977 few people would have enjoyed this book. However, with the investigation of Babe Didrikson's life and a similar revealing biography of Olympian Jesse Owens, there is a renewed interest in not only knowing the successes of an athlete's life, but understanding the social, political, and cultural forces that shaped the athlete in their successes and failures in both athletics and life.

Oriard concludes that while most autobiographies of athletes are "generally regarded as slight amusements, no more consequential than newspaper gossip columns," autobiographies of Black athletes have "an inescapable political dimension, whether or not the author chooses to acknowledge that reality." Instead of serving simply as a document of their sporting experience, these autobiographies are accounts of the self-fashioning of Black athletes, as dictated by current racial politics as well as by more narrowly personal intentions."[9]

Wilma may not have been thinking about making a political statement with her book. She may have been more concerned with simply leaving an account of her life and her athletic accomplishments. Soon after the publication of the book, a made for television movie was produced by Olympic film maker, Bud Greenspan, who was a big fan of Wilma's from her days of competition. At the time of the television movie, track and field was not a popular subject for Hollywood.[10] There had been no biographical features of an African American track and field athlete until the story of Wilma hit the small screen.

Wilma did not appear in the film, but she did serve as a consultant during the making of the movie. Despite the movie being based on her book, Wilma did not profit from the film. A young Denzel Washington appeared as Wilma's boyfriend, Robert Eldridge, and Cicely Tyson appeared as Wilma's mother, Blanche Rudolph. The most redeeming feature of Greenspan's film was his usage of the actual Olympic footage, showing Wilma winning all three races.

The movie was largely based on Wilma's book and did not serve to fill in any gaps that she did not discuss in her book. In fact, while it corrects some errors from her book, it includes other errors. For example, it has Wilma running at Tennessee State in the summer of 1955, but then has the AAU championship track meet in Philadelphia and Wilma winning all her races (that happened the next year). It skips over the 1956 Olympics entirely. While it focuses more on her relationship with Robert, as well as her relationship with her father, than in her book, it also shows Coach Temple as very supportive of her pregnancy, and it appears as if Wilma told Coach Temple before talking with her parents. The movie ends with her calling her family from Rome to talk with them after her three victories and her father excited to have her come home. Text appears on the screen and the reader is informed that Wilma's father died later that year, and Wilma and Robert got married later that year, and were now living in Tennessee with their four children (according to her own autobiography, she and Robert did not marry until 1963).

It is a classic "rags to riches" (though Wilma did not get rich, she did achieve success at the Olympics) story beginning with her childhood struggles to walk and resulting in her track and field record accomplishment of three gold medals at the 1960 Olympic Games. It does not go beyond her Olympic success, which serves the purpose of highlighting her remarkable achievements, but fails to reveal her post-Olympic struggles that she briefly discusses in her book. Just as many people might not have been interested in reading a book that included her disappointments, perhaps the viewing audience would not have found inspiration from seeing her succeed and then struggle in her post-Olympic life.

Despite the various versions of Wilma's life, whether they appeared in newspapers, magazines, a television movie, or even her own autobiography, clearly her accomplishments merit celebration. Wilma Rudolph's story is more than the races she won and world records she established. It is the story of a young woman who overcame tremendous obstacles that should have kept her from ever experiencing athletic success, and yet she is the epitome of triumph. Regardless of any troubles she may have experienced later in life, Wilma's life remains as a testament to her ability to "make the best" of her athletic achievements during a time period that did not celebrate African American women, in athletics and in American society. Her failures and successes reveal a human being who is multidimensional. Not just a runner, not just a mother, not just an Olympian—Wilma is a forgotten pioneer. In all of her efforts to control the ways her life was to be remembered, it is best to consider that her motive was simply that—to be remembered—and to be remembered for what she overcame and accomplished despite all the odds.

NOTES

1. Other books written about Wilma Rudolph have focused primarily on juvenile readers. These books include: Tom Biracree, *Wilma Rudolph* (New York: Chelsea House, 1988); Kathleen Krull, *Wilma Unlimited: How Wilma Rudolph Became the World's Fastest Woman* (San Diego: Harcourt Brace, 1996); Amy Ruth, *Wilma Rudolph* (Minneapolis: Lerner Publications Company, 1999).

2. Michael Oriard, "Autobiographies," in *African Americans in Sport: Volume 1*, ed. David K. Wiggins (Armonk, NY: M.E. Sharpe, 2004), 17.

3. Oriard, "Autobiographies," *African Americans in Sport*, 16.

4. Oriard, "Autobiographies," *African Americans in Sport*, 16.

5. Cindy Himes Gissendanner, "African American Women Olympians: The Impact of Race, Gender, and Class Ideologies, 1932–1968," *Research Quarterly for Exercise and Sport* 67(2): 179.

6. "What ever happened to Wilma Rudolph?" *EBONY* (February 1984): 84.

7. Babe Didrikson Zaharias as told to Harry Paxton, *This life I've Led: My Autobiography* (New York: A.S. Barnes, 1955); Susan Cayleff, *Babe: The Life and Legend of Babe Didrikson Zaharias* (Urbana: University of Illinois Press, 1995).

8. Oriard, "Autobiographies," *African Americans in Sport*, 16.

9. Oriard, "Autobiographies," *African Americans in Sport*, 17.

10. *Wilma* (1977). Directed by Bud Greenspan. NBC, Cappy Productions.

Chapter 12

THE LEGACY OF WILMA RUDOLPH—FROM EVELYN ASHFORD TO MARION JONES

There she was, with the whole world focused on her. And wasn't it wonderful. Here was someone who looked like me, and she'd done something that everybody celebrated.[1]

—Anita DeFrantz

The triumph can't be had without the struggle. And I know what struggle is. I have spent a lifetime sharing what it has meant to be a woman first in the world of sports so that other young women have a chance to reach their dreams.[2]

—Wilma Rudolph

Wilma Rudolph made history when she became the first American woman to win three gold medals in track and field at the 1960 Olympic Games. She was the first of many great African American female sprinters who would follow her path to success. In the years following Wilma's terrific performance, other Tigerbelles would find success at the Olympic Games, such as Edith McGuire and Wyomia Tyus. As more colleges offered track and field programs, Tennessee State no longer dominated the ranks of the Olympic teams. American women lost their domination in the Olympic sprints failing to win a track and field gold medal in the 1972 Munich Olympics and the 1976 Montreal Olympics; in fact, between the two teams, they won only two silver medals, both in the 4x400-meter relay. Evelyn Ashford emerged as the sprinter of the 1980s, along with Valerie Brisco-Hooks, followed by sister-in-laws Florence Griffith-Joyner and Jackie Joyner-Kersee in the 1990s, then Gail Devers, Gwen Torrance, and most recently Marion Jones. All have traveled the path first blazed by Wilma at the 1960 Olympic Games.

Wilma's legacy had already been established before her untimely death in 1994. She had been inducted into the Black Sports Hall of Fame (1973), the U.S. Track and Field Hall of Fame (1974), the National Women's Hall of Fame (1980), and the U.S. Olympic Hall of Fame (1983). Even though she had never competed in National Collegiate Athletic Association (NCAA) sponsored women's championships, Wilma received the NCAA's Silver Anniversary Award in 1990. (The NCAA did not govern women's championship events until the 1980s.) A year later, she was presented with the Crown Royal Achievement Award for "demonstrating courage and perseverance in overcoming physical problems."[3] Thirty years after her Olympic victories, Wilma was still being celebrated for her childhood victory over polio. In June 1993, Wilma, along with Arnold Palmer, Kareem Abdul-Jabbar, Muhammad Ali, and Ted Williams, were honored by President Bill Clinton as "the Great Ones" at the first National Sports Awards.

In the months preceding her premature death in 1994, Wilma won the National Woman's Hall of Fame award, had a section of Route 79 in Clarksville renamed Wilma Rudolph Boulevard, and was awarded two honorary degrees. Only nine months after Wilma's death, Tennessee State, on August 11, 1995, dedicated its new six-story dormitory the Wilma G. Rudolph Residence Center. On October 13, 1995, Tennessee State's annual Edward S. Temple Seminars in Society and Sports named their annual luncheon the Wilma Rudolph Memorial Luncheon. A black marble marker was placed on her grave in Clarksville's Foster Memorial Garden Cemetery by the Wilma Rudolph Memorial Commission on November 21, 1995. After raising close to $80,000 to commission a statue of Wilma, a life-sized bronze statute of Wilma Rudolph was completed for the city of Clarksville, Tennessee, by artist Howard A. Brown in April 1996. In 1997, Governor Don Sundquist proclaimed June 23 as Wilma Rudolph Day in Tennessee. At the end of the millennium, ESPN ranked Wilma number 41 on ESPN's list of the twentieth century's greatest athletes. Her amazing triple win at the 1960 Olympic Games was selected by ESPN as the second most important event in women's sports in the twentieth century, behind Billie Jean King's 1973 victory over Bobby Riggs at the Houston Astrodome on national television. In 2003, Clarksville erected a historical marker at the intersections of Old Trenton Boulevard and Wilma Rudolph Boulevard honoring their hometown hero. (She had once lived on Trenton Boulevard.) Wilma was finally getting her due, long after her amazing Olympic victories and too late for her to enjoy. A 23-cent stamp in the Distinguished American Series was issued by the U.S. Postal Service honoring Wilma Rudolph in 2004. The stamp's release was celebrated at the 2004 U.S. Track and Field Olympic Trials in Sacramento. A Second Day Ceremony was held in Clarksville to honor the woman who put the small Tennessee town on the map. Wilma's stamp was only the fifth in the Distinguished American Series.

By the end of the 1960s, Black women in track and field were making their mark in terms of athletics style and feminine style, and Wilma was at the forefront of this movement. Anita Verschoth, for *Sports Illustrated* wrote, "Like a cloud of newly emerged butterflies, they appeared out of nowhere—which is where women track and field athletes seem to spend time between national championships—to provide a kaleidoscope of beauty and color that even the local Fourth of July fireworks could not match."[4] Moreover, many remarked that their femininity had helped to dispel many of the misconceptions about women and sport. "If the meet emphasized one thing, it was that a girl no longer has to look like a boy to compete in track and field, a development that becomes more obvious every year."[5] By the end of the decade, women had successfully begun to shape the image of women's track and field into one that included grace, beauty and certainly femininity. This is one of Wilma's significant legacies in the sport.

Beyond the changing view of womanhood and sport, Wilma was part of a group that altered American attitudes regarding the race of competitors. As the U.S. women rose to the top of international track and field, African American female athletes received more attention, more respect, and were recognized as major contributors to American sporting success. Coach Ed Temple commented on witnessing this shift from those women to our women. "The word was 'our,' and it meant that girls in shorts and spikes were no longer a subject to be avoided in gracious conversation. 'I've heard those television people before,' said Temple. 'It was always 'the girls.' But when they started beating the Russians in Los Angeles, you know what the announcer called them? He called them 'our girls.' "[6] Wilma was a vital part of the shifting attitudes about African American women in track and field which spread to other sports and throughout society. She was crucial to the acceptance of Black women being viewed as "Americans" simply due to their ability to run faster than their Soviet Union competitors. Their success was valued by Americans for what it represented about the United States. Similar to the symbolic roles Joe

Louis and Jesse Owens held in using sport to become more "American," Wilma and her African American teammates were able to do the same 25 years later for African American women.

Since the 1960s, many African American women have dominated the rosters of America's Olympic track and field teams. Few have matched Wilma's 1960 trio of gold medals or her popularity in the American consciousness. Tigerbelles Edith McGuire and Wyomia Tyus both won gold medals in the Olympic sprints in the 1960s, replacing Wilma, but never matching her triple crown or her world class speed. Evelyn Ashford first competed in the 1976 Montreal Olympic Games and remembered first hearing about Wilma Rudolph when she was 11 or 12 years old; "when I saw her on TV I knew I wanted to be like her."[7] Ashford admired Rudolph for her passion, pride, and dignity. Ashford won two gold medals in 1984, in the 100-meter dash and the 4x100-meter relay, and at the next Olympiad, won silver medals in both events. In 1984, sprinter Valerie Brisco-Hooks became the second American woman to win three track and field gold medals at the Olympics, when she swept the 200-meter and 400-meter dashes, and the 4x400-meter relay at the 1984 Olympic Games in Los Angeles, California. Twenty-four years after Wilma's victories, Brisco-Hooks had matched the accomplishments, but did not receive the same media coverage as Wilma. There had been very little expectations of Brisco-Hooks at the 1984 Games and after her three wins, but like Wilma she did not earn major endorsements or even much publicity.[8] Much of this was thought to be due to the changing popularity of track and field in the United States.

However, only four years later, at the 1988 Olympic Games in Seoul, Korea, the feat was matched when Florence Griffith-Joyner won three gold medals in the 100-meter and 200-meter dashes, and the 4x400-meter relay. She had shattered the world record in the 100-meters in a blazing 10.49 seconds, an unbelievably fast time and one that raised suspicions of steroids. Her threesome of gold medals was viewed completely different than her teammate Valerie Brisco-Hooks' accomplishment at the previous Olympic Games. "Flo Jo" was a media sensation and was on the cover of *Newsweek, Time, Life, Ebony,* and *Jet.* She received offers from modeling agencies, film producers, and fashion magazines. Similar to the media coverage of Wilma in 1960, the French press called Flo Jo "la tigresse noire" (the black tiger), and the emphasis was on her feminine appearance, including her one-legged running suits and long fingernails, also very consistent with the media coverage of the 1960s. However, unlike Wilma and other track athletes of the 1960s, Flo Jo had the opportunity to earn money through running. Track and field had changed their amateur rulings and now allowed for appearance money. Flo Jo's triple-crown catapulted her into the highest earning bracket for Olympic athletes.[9] Wilma was able to see Flo Jo match her medal count and was thrilled to see her run to victory; "It was a great thrill for me to see. I thought I'd never get to see that. Florence Griffith Joyner—every time she ran, I ran."

Bob Kersee had been Flo Jo's coach at California State University, Northridge, and also coached his wife, Jackie Joyner-Kersee, who had won two gold medals at the 1988 Seoul Olympics in the long jump and heptathlon. Coach Kersee credits Rudolph as the greatest influence for African-American women athletes that he knows. Jackie Joyner-Kersee, who eventually won a total of six Olympic medals, said this of Wilma, "She was always in my corner. If I had a problem, I could call her at home. It was like talking to someone you knew for a lifetime." Jackie Joyner-Kersee, who many people consider to be the greatest female athlete of all time, competed in four Olympic Games and at one point of her career earned close to $1 million a year. Sprinter Gwen Torrance, also an Olympic gold medalist in the springs, who in high school feared seeming too masculine if she wore sneakers and gym shorts, signed a sneaker contract with Nike that had performance bonuses that added up to $3 million.[10] Unfortunately Wilma never enjoyed this kind of financial success, but her performances opened the doors for these women simply by establishing an image for young Black girls to emulate.

More recently, Marion Jones earned the title of America's greatest sprinter. Prior to the 2000 Olympic Games in Sydney, Australia, Marion boldly proclaimed that she was aiming to win five gold medals, bettering the three won by Wilma Rudolph and the four gold medals won by Jesse Owens at the 1936 Berlin Olympic Games. Though she did not win the five gold medals, she did win five medals; three gold medals (in the 100-meter, 200-meter and 4x400-meter relay) and two bronze medals (long jump and 4x100-meter relay), the most medals won by a female track and field athlete in one single Olympiad. When asked if she is the greatest female track star ever, Marion was humble enough to respond, "No, you need longevity and consistency to be considered the greatest. I haven't even broken world records yet. In 10 or 15 years, we can then sit down and think about how great it all was. But not now."[11]

Marion also enjoyed plenty of media coverage, though much of it also focused on her femininity. Female athletes still have to contend with stereotypes and expectations related to their gender and sport participation. Donna Lopiano, executive director of the Women's Sports Foundation, stated that "with the glut of distractions we have today, it's harder for Marion Jones to shine than it was for Wilma Rudolph. Today, it's all about exposure of logo and brand and the exploitation of celebrity. Marion has to decide if she wants to be Tiger Woods. Can she be that? Yes. Does the American public want a female sports icon of that largeness? Yes, definitely."[12] Despite Lopiano's suggestion that it is harder for Marion Jones to shine than it was for Wilma, the reality is that Marion Jones, because of the advances made by Wilma Rudolph and other African American female athletes, is able to profit from her track and field talents in ways that Wilma Rudolph could only have imagined in her wildest dreams. That said, Marion Jones has recently been pillaged in the press for allegations that she took performance enhancing drugs and she has been unable to match her 2000 Olympic Games performance.

In her autobiography, in one of her rare moments of reflection on the impact of race, Wilma revealed a consciousness about her status as a Black female athlete in America. She felt as if they were "on the bottom rung of the ladder in American sports."[13] She recognized that track and field was one of the only sports where Black women could even participate and wondered why there weren't more Black female golfers or tennis players. Reflecting back on her own situation, she stated that once the Olympics were over, there was no place for Black female athletes to go and pursue their sport. She pushed for a professional track circuit that paid the athletes beyond travel expenses. Eventually there was a professional track and field circuit, but Wilma never benefited from the professionalization of her sport. In a 1973 interview, she said that she had been asked to run as a pro, but that by then her interests were with her family and in developing other champions.[14] She said she did not feel the women's liberation movement was relevant to her as they seemed to be encouraging women to leave the home and get jobs. She argued that Black women had always been working, so getting a job was not the answer to changing the status of Black women. She addressed the racial tensions within the women's liberation movement, stating that it was "nothing but a bunch of White women who had certain lifestyles and who want to change those life-styles,"[15] and she mentioned that these women did not want men to open their doors or light their cigarettes. Again, she argued that Black women had been opening their own doors for years. Her issues with the women's liberation movement were both about their failure to address the inclusion of Black women in the movement, but also her feelings which opposed the feminism movement, which may have included lesbians, and her own homophobia. She does not explicitly indicate this except in her coded language, such as "certain life-styles." Her thoughts indicate the clashes between the sexism and racism that permeated American society during the late 1960s and early 1970s.

In the decade before her death, Wilma talked about her new attitude, perhaps as a response to some of the personal problems and employment troubles she had experienced. She was in the process of reinventing herself. "No one, I've discovered, comes ringing the door to say, 'We're looking for Wilma Rudolph to do some work for us.' I had to ring my own bell. You can do that, and it's a lie if anyone says you can't. You have to get into the world and make your own accomplishments. And as with anything you do, you have to sacrifice."[16] It seemed as though Wilma was finally ready to examine herself and her own accountability for some of the difficult aspects of her post-Olympic life.

What gave Wilma Rudolph joy throughout her life was her family and service to others. At the time of her death, she had four children, eight grandchildren, and over 100 nieces and nephews. Despite the hardships she faced as a child and then as an adult after her Olympic successes, the tough times never seemed to keep her down. She claimed that her greatest accomplishment in life was creating the Wilma Rudolph Foundation; "If I have anything to leave, the foundation is my legacy."[17] She often stated that she wanted to be remembered for more than her feats on the track. Rather, she hoped to be remembered for her contributions to the lives of young people. Throughout her short life, Wilma Rudolph overcame tremendous odds to live a remarkable life.

As the 20th child in a poor African American family living in the segregated town of Clarksville, Tennessee, Wilma suffered numerous childhood illnesses. Polio was her earliest opponent and left her partially paralyzed. With the love and support of her family, Wilma was able to walk without a brace when she was 11, opening the doors for a new and more active life. Segregation was another barrier. Throughout her childhood, she attended segregated schools and competed in segregated athletic events. First she was a basketball star and then the track became her home. Basketball had also been segregated, but track offered Wilma her first opportunities to compete in integrated competitions. She became the youngest member of the U.S. women's Olympic track and field team and won a bronze medal in the 4x100-meter relay at the 1956 Olympic Games in Melbourne, Australia.

Wilma's next obstacle was becoming a teen mother, which kept her out of athletics for a year. Many women would have quit then, but not Wilma, she was just getting started. As one of Coach Ed Temple's Tigerbelles, Wilma won seven national Athletic Amateur Union sprint titles and became the first American woman to win three track and field gold medals at the 1960 Olympic Games. She won numerous awards for her Olympic accomplishments and continued to compete as an amateur athlete for the next two years in national and international competitions. She was one of America's greatest weapons against the Soviet Union's dominance in track and field. She continued to win more awards for her accomplishments on the track, but retired before the next Olympic Games in Tokyo, Japan. Olympic filmmaker Bud Greenspan thought Wilma was 25 years before her time.

Wilma's greatest barriers lay ahead in battling the complex and multiple ways that African American women face both racism and sexism. Multiply this with Wilma's position as an Olympic champion who was valued for her celebrity status, but not her abilities to contribute her ideas, whether it was because she was a woman in a man's world, or an African American in a country that was struggling with integration. She had a difficult time holding on to jobs and making enough money to take care of her family. Still, she continued to serve others through a variety of positions that focused on developing the talents of young people who did not have the economic resources to pay for training. Wilma started her own foundation which aimed to serve the development of youth from lower-income backgrounds. She never forgot her Tennessee roots.

Wilma's last opponent was a disease that took her life at a time when she should have been enjoying her children and grandchildren and continuing to work in her community. America had changed their ideas about women in sport, about African Americans in society, and Wilma died too soon for a new generation of Americans to appreciate her accomplishments on and off the track. Bud Greenspan, the Olympic filmmaker who produced the film version of Wilma's life in 1977, said that Wilma was the "Jesse Owens of women's track and field, and like Jesse, she changed the sport for all time. She became the benchmark for little black girls to aspire."[18] At her funeral, teammate Mae Faggs Starr said that Wilma had really set the stage for Black women to compete on the national and international stage; "She showed that we could beat the world."[19] In the days following her death, there were impressive tributes and a retelling of her amazing heroic story of overcoming so many barriers. In a tribute to Wilma, New York Times columnist Ira Berkow wrote, "Her legacy, her inspiring story, is a model of all the clichés turned truisms in sports. For boys as well as girls. For any color. From any culture. With any handicap." He concluded with a quote from Wilma; "When I was running, I had the sense of freedom, of running in the wind. I never forgot all the years when I was a little girl and not able to

be involved. When I ran, I felt like a butterfly."[20] Hers is a story of struggle and adversity, of courage and determination, and ultimately one of
great success. Her flaws and fragilities only contribute to her humanness.
Wilma Rudolph's legacy lives on into the twenty-first century as one of
America's greatest stories.

NOTES

1. Brad Herzog, *The Sports 100: The One Hundred Most Important People in
American Sports History* (New York: Macmillan, 1995), 241. DeFrantz was an
Olympic medalist in rowing at the 1976 Olympic Games in Montreal and is cur-
rently a member of the International Olympic Committee.

2. Anne Jannette Johnson, *Great Women in Sports* (Minneapolis: Visible Ink
Press, 1996), 405.

3. "Athletes Honored for Perseverance," *New York Times*, 11 October 1991,
B12.

4. Anita Verschoth, "Some Dashing Dolls Debut in Dayton," *Sports
Illustrated*, 14 July 1969, 20.

5. Verschoth, "Some Dashing Dolls Debut in Dayton," 20.

6. Tom C. Brody, "At Last the Girls Are Ours," *Sports Illustrated*, 17 August
1964, 68.

7. Evelyn Ashford, "In her tracks," *New York Times*, 1 January 1995,
SM37.

8. Peter Alfano, "3 Golds Change Little in Brisco-Hooks Life," *New York
Times*, 25 January 1985, A19.

9. Michael D. Davis, *Black American Women in Olympic Track and Field*
(Jefferson, NC: McFarland & Company, Inc., 1992), 67–71. Also see Frank
Litsky, "Griffith Joyner Wins More than Gold," *New York Times*, 30 September
1988, A16.

10. Jere Longman, "How the Women Won," *New York Times*, 23 June 1996.

11. Ira Berkow, "Sports of the Times; Years Later, Jones feels a link to Owens,"
New York Times, 9 February 2001.

12. Thomas Hackett, "Speed Demon," *New York Times*, 14 May 2000.

13. Wilma Rudolph, with Martin Ralbovsky, *Wilma: The Story of Wilma
Rudolph* (New York: Signet, 1977), 167.

14. Joan Ryan, *Contributions of Women: Sports* (Minneapolis, MN: Dillon
Press, Inc., 1975), 63.

15. Rudolph, *Wilma*, 169.

16. Zenobia Jonell Gerald, "Rudolph's Free to Run a Winning Streak,"
Sacramento Bee, 2 June 1981, B5.

17. Frank Litsky, "Wilma Rudolph, Star of the 1960 Olympics, Dies at 54,"
New York Times, 13 November 1994, 53.

18. Litsky, "Wilma Rudolph, Star of the 1960 Olympics, Dies at 54," 53.

19. William C. Rhoden, "The End of a Winding Road," *New York Times*, 19 November 1994, 31.

20. Ira Berkow, "Sports of the Times; Forever the Regal Champion," *New York Times*, 13 November 1994, S9.

Appendix

PERFORMANCES OF AFRICAN AMERICAN WOMEN IN OLYMPIC TRACK AND FIELD

Year	Location	Athlete	Event	Performance
1932	Los Angeles, California, USA	Tidye Pickett Louise Stokes	Both were members of the 4x100-m relay.	Neither competed in the relay; they were both replaced by White runners.
1936	Berlin, Germany	Tidye Pickett Louise Stokes	80-m hurdles 4x100-m relay	Injured in the semifinals Replaced by a White runner
1940	Cancelled due to World War II			
1944	Cancelled due to World War II			
1948	London, England	Alice Coachman	High jump	1st place; 5' 6 ½" feet; Olympic Record
		Mae Faggs	200-m dash	Did not qualify for finals
		Nell Jackson	200-m dash	Did not qualify for finals
		Theresa Manuel	80-m hurdles; Javelin	Did not qualify for finals Did not qualify for finals
		Audrey Patterson	200-m dash	3rd place; 25.2 seconds
		Emma Reed	High jump	Did not qualify for finals
		Bernice Robinson	60-m hurdles	Did not qualify for finals
		Lillian Young	60-m hurdles	Did not qualify for finals
		Faggs, Jackson, Evelyn Lawler, Jean Patton	4x100-m relay	Did not qualify for finals

Year	Location	Athlete	Event	Result
1952	Helsinki, Finland	Mae Faggs	100-m dash	6th place
		Faggs, Catherine Hardy, Barbara Jones	4x100-m relay	Did not qualify for finals; 45.9 seconds
1956	Melbourne, Australia	Earlene Brown	Shot put; Discus	Did not qualify for finals / Did not qualify for finals
		Isabelle Daniels	100-m dash	4th place; 11.8 seconds
1956	Melbourne, Australia	Mae Faggs	100-m dash; 200 m dash	Did not qualify for finals / Did not qualify for finals
		Margaret Matthews	Long jump	Did not qualify for finals
		Mildred McDaniel	High jump	1st place; 5' 9 ¼" feet; World Record
		Wilma Rudolph	200-m dash	Did not qualify for finals
		Willye White	Long jump	2nd place; 19' 11 ½" feet
		Lucinda Williams	100-m dash	Did not qualify for finals
		Faggs, Matthews, Rudolph, Daniels	4x100-m relay	3rd place; 44.9 seconds
1960	Rome, Italy	Earlene Brown	Shot put; Discus	3rd place; 53' 10 1/4" feet / 6th place
		Shirley Crowder	80-m hurdles	Did not qualify for finals
		Barbara Jones	100-m dash	11.7 seconds
		Neomia Rodgers	High jump	14th place
		Wilma Rudolph	100-m dash; 200 m dash;	1st place; 11.0 seconds; World Record / 1st place; 24.0 seconds

Year	Location	Athlete	Event	Performance
1960	Rome, Italy	Willye White	Long jump	16th place
		Lucinda Williams	100-m dash;	Did not qualify for finals
			200-m dash	Did not qualify for finals
		Martha Hudson, Williams, Jones, Rudolph	4x100-m relay	1st place; 44.5 seconds
1964	Tokyo, Japan	Estelle Baskerville	High jump	Did not qualify for finals
		Rosie Bonds	80-m hurdles	8th place; 10.6 seconds
		Earlene Brown	Shot put	12th place; 48' 6 ¼" feet
		Terrezene Brown	High jump	14th place; no mark
		Edith McGuire	100-m dash;	2nd place; 11.6 seconds
			200-m dash	1st place; 23.0 seconds; Olympic Record
		Eleanor Montegomery	High jump	8th place; 1.71 meters
		Cherrie Parish	100-m hurdles	Did not qualify for finals
		Debbie Thompson	100-m dash	Did not qualify for finals
		Kim Turner	80-m hurdles	Did not qualify for finals
		Wyomia Tyus	100-m dash	1st place; 11.4 seconds
		Marilyn White	100-m dash	3rd place; 11.6 seconds
		Willye White	Long jump	12th place; 19' 8 ¼" feet
		Tyus, McGuire, W. White, M. White	4x100-m relay	2nd place; 43.9 seconds

Year	Location	Athlete	Event	Result
1968	Mexico City, Mexico	Estelle Baskerville	High jump	Did not qualify for finals
		Doris Brown	800-m run	5th place; 2:03.9
		Barbara Ferrell	100-m dash;	2nd place; 11.1 seconds
			200-m dash	4th place; 22.9 seconds
		Madeline Manning	800-m run	1st place; 2:00.9 minutes; Olympic Record
		Eleanor Montegomery	High jump	Did not qualify for finals
		Mamie Rallins	80-m hurdles	Did not qualify for finals
		Wyomia Tyus	100-m dash;	1st place; 11.0 seconds; World Record
			200-m dash	6th place; 23.0 seconds
		Tyus, Ferrell, Margaret Bailes, Mildrette Netter	4x100-m relay	1st place; 42.8 seconds
1972	Munich, Germany	Iris Davis	100-m dash	4th place; 11.32 seconds
		Mable Ferguson	400-m run	5th place; 51.96 seconds
		Gail Fitzgerald	Pentathlon	Did not qualify for finals
		Madeline Manning	800-m run	Did not qualify for finals
		Mamie Rallins	80-m hurdles	Did not qualify for finals
		Martha Watson, Mattiline Render, Mildrette Netter, Iris Davis	4x100-m relay	4th place; 43.39 seconds
		Mable Ferguson, Madeline Manning, Cheryl Toussaint	4x400-m relay	2nd place; 3:25.2 minutes

Year	Location	Athlete	Event	Performance
1976	Montreal, Canada	Evelyn Ashford	100-m dash	5th place; 11.24 seconds
		Rosalyn Bryant	400-m run	5th place; 50.65 seconds
		Chandra Cheeseborough	100-m dash	6th place; 11.31 seconds
		Gail Fitzgerald	Pentathlon	Did not qualify for finals
		Shelia Ingram	400-m run	6th place; 59.90 seconds
		Pam Jiles	200-m dash	Did not qualify for finals
		Madeline Manning	800-m run	Did not qualify for finals
			800-m run	Did not qualify for finals
		Brenda Morehead	100-m dash;	Did not qualify for finals
			200-m dash	Did not qualify for finals
		Debra Sapenter	400-m run	8th place; 51.66 seconds
		Martha Watson, Ashford, Debra Armstrong, Cheeseborough	4x100-m relay	7th place; 43.35 seconds
		Sapenter, Ingram, Jiles, Bryant	4x400-m relay	2nd place; 3:22.81 minutes
1980	Moscow, Soviet Union	United States boycotted as a political protest regarding Soviet invasion of Afghanistan		

1984	Jodi Anderson	Long jump	Did not qualify for finals
Los Angeles, California, USA	Evelyn Ashford	100-m dash	1st place; 10.97 seconds
	Jeanette Bolden	100-m dash	4th place; 11.25 seconds
	Valerie Brisco-Hooks	200-m dash;	1st place; 21.81 seconds
		400-m run	1st place; 48.83 seconds
	Alice Brown	100-m dash	2nd place; 11.13 seconds
	Judi Brown	400-m hurdles	2nd place; 55.20 seconds
	Robin Campbell	800-m run	Did not qualify for finals
	Chandra Cheeseborough	400-m run	2nd place; 49.05 seconds
	Diane Dixon	100-m dash	Did not qualify for finals
	Benita Fitzgerald-Brown	100-m hurdles	1st place; 12.84 seconds
	Kim Gallagher	800-m run	2nd place; 1:58.63 minutes
	Missy Gerald	800-m run	Did not qualify for finals
	Randy Givins	200-m dash	6th place; 22.36 seconds
	Florence Griffith-Joyner	200-m dash	2nd place; 22.04 seconds
	Jackie Joyner-Kersee	Long jump;	5th place; 22' 2 ½"
		Heptathlon	2nd place; 6,385 points
	Lillie Leatherwood	400-m run	3rd place; 50.25 seconds
	Carol Lewis	Long jump	9th place; 21' 1 ¼" feet
	LaShon Nedd	400-m run	Did not qualify for finals
	Pamela Page	100-m hurdles	8th place; 13.40 seconds

Year	Location	Athlete	Event	Performance
1984	Los Angeles, California, USA	Angela Thacher	Long jump	4th place; 22' 3" feet
		Kim Turner	100-m hurdles	2nd place; 12.88 seconds
		A. Brown, Bolden, Cheeseborough, Ashford	4x100-m relay	1st place; 41.65 seconds
		Brisco-Hooks, Cheeseborough, Leatherwood, Sheri Howard	4x400-m relay	1st place; 3:18.29 minutes
1988	Seoul, Korea	Evelyn Ashford	100-m dash	2nd place; 10.57 seconds
		Joetta Clark-Diggs	800-m run	Did not qualify for finals; 2:00.88 minutes
		Gail Devers	100-m hurdles	Did not qualify for finals
		Kim Gallagher	800-m run	3rd place; 1:56.91 minutes
		Florence Griffith-Joyner	100-m dash;	1st place; 10.54 seconds
			200-m dash	1st place; 21.34 seconds
		Regina Jacobs	1500-m run	Did not qualify for finals; 4:18.09 minutes
		Jackie Joyner-Kersee	Long jump;	1st place; 24' 3 ½" feet; Olympic Record
			Heptathlon	1st place; 7,291 points; World Record
			100-m hurdles	Qualified for finals

Lavonna Martin	Relay alternate	18th place
Jearl Miles	Shot put	16th place
Connie Price-Smith	Discus	
Ashford, Alice Brown, Shelia Echols, Griffith-Joyner	4x100-m relay	1st place; 41.98 seconds
Valerie Brisco-Hooks, Diane Dixon, Denean Howard-Hill, Griffith-Joyner	4x400-m relay	2nd place; 3:15.51 minutes

Year	City	Name	Event	Result
1992	Barcelona, Spain	Tonya Buford-Bailey	400-m hurdles	Did not qualify for finals
		Joetta Clark-Diggs	800-m run	7th place; 1:58.06 minutes
		Gail Devers	100-m dash	1st place; 10.82 seconds
			100-m hurdles	5th place; 12.75 seconds
		Sandra Farmer-Patrick	400-m hurdles	2nd place; 53.69 seconds
		Regina Jacobs	1500-m run	Did not qualify for finals; 4:21.55 minutes
		Jackie Joyner-Kersee	Long jump	3rd place; 23' 2 ¼" feet
			heptathlon	1st place; 7044 points
		LaVonna Martin	100-m hurdles	2nd place; 12.69 seconds
		Jearl Miles	400-m	5th place in semis

Year	Location	Athlete	Event	Performance
1992	Barcelona, Spain	Connie Price-Smith	Shot put	Did not qualify for finals
			Discus	20th place; 192' 5" feet
		Lynda Tolbert	100-m hurdles	4th place; 12.75 seconds
		Gwen Torrence	200-m dash	1st place; 21.81 seconds
		Janeene Vickers	400-m hurdles	3rd place; 54.31 seconds
		Evelyn Ashford, Esther Jones, Carlette Guidry-White, Gwen Torrence	4x100-m relay	1st place; 42.11 seconds
		Natasha Kaiser, Gwen Torrence, Jearl Miles, Rochelle Stevens	4x400-m relay	2nd place; 3:20.92 minutes
1996	Atlanta, Georgia, USA	Kim Batten	400-m hurdles	2nd place; 53.08 seconds
		Tonya Buford-Bailey	400-m hurdles	3rd place; 53.22 seconds
		Joetta Clark-Diggs	800-m run	Did not qualify for the finals
		Gail Devers	100-m dash	1st place; 10.94 seconds
			100-m hurdles	4th place; 12.66 seconds
		Lynda Goode	100-m hurdles	8th place; 13.11 seconds
		Kim Graham	400-m	Did not qualify for the finals; 51.13 seconds
		Shelia Hudson	Triple jump	10th place
		Regina Jacobs	1500-m run	10th place; 4:07.21 minutes
		Jackie Joyner-Kersee	Long jump	3rd place; 22' 11 3/4" feet

		Jearl Miles	400-m run	5th place
		Connie Price-Smith	Shot put	5th place; 63' ¾" feet
		Gwen Torrance	100-m dash	3rd place; 10.96 seconds
		Shana Williams	Long jump	Did not qualify for finals
		Chryste Gaines, Devers, Inger Miller, Torrance	4x100-m relay	1st place; 41.95 seconds
		Rochelle Stevens, Maicel Malone, Kim Graham, Miles	4x400-m relay	1st place; 3:20.91 minutes
2000	Sydney, Australia	Kim Batten	400-m hurdles	Did not qualify for finals; 55.73 seconds
		Torya Buford-Bailey	400-m hurdles	Did not qualify for finals; 57.02 seconds
		Dawn Burrell	Long jump	11th place; 6.38 meters
		Shelia Burrell	Heptathlon	26th place; 5345 points
		Hazel Clark	800-m run	7th place; 1:58.75 minutes
		Joetta Clark-Diggs	800-m run	Did not qualify for finals; 2:04.12
		Latasha Colander-Richardson	400-m run	Did not qualify for finals; 52.06 seconds

Year	Location	Athlete	Event	Performance
2000	Sydney, Australia	Michelle Collins	400-m run	53.66 seconds in 1st round
		Gail Devers	100-m hurdles	Injured in race; did not finish
		Torri Edwards	200-m dash	Did not qualify for finals; 23.06 seconds
		Dawn Ellerbee	Hammer	7th place; 219' 2" feet
		Chryste Gaines	100-m dash	Did not qualify for finals; 11.23 seconds
		Nicole Gamble	Triple jump	Did not qualify for finals; 13.33 meters
		Sandra Glover	400-m hurdles	Did not qualify for finals; 54.98 seconds
		Monique Hennagan	400-m	51.73 seconds in 1st round
		Shelia Hudson	Triple jump	Did not compete
		Regina Jacobs	1500-m run	Did not compete
		Sharon Jewel	100-m hurdles	Did not qualify for finals; 12.78 seconds
		Marion Jones	100-m dash	1st place; 10.75 seconds
			200-m dash	1st place; 21.87 seconds
			Long jump	3rd place; 22' 8 ½" feet
		Jearl Miles	400-m run;	Did not qualify for finals
			800-m run	5th place in semis; 1:59.44 minutes
		Inger Miller	100-m dash;	Withdrew due to injury
			200-m dash	Withdrew due to injury
		Melissa Morrison	100-m hurdles	3rd place; 12.76 seconds
		DeDee Nathan	Heptathlon	9th place; 6150 points

124

Year	Location	Name	Event	Result
		Nanceen Perry	200-m dash	Did not qualify for finals; 23.16 seconds
		Connie Price-Smith	Shot put	Did not qualify for finals
		Shana Williams	Long jump	Did not qualify for finals; 6.44 meters
		Chryste Gaines, Torri Edwards, Nanceen Perry, Marion Jones	4x100-m relay	3rd place; 42.20 seconds
		Jearl Miles, Monique Hennagan, Marion Jones, La Tasha Colander-Richardson	4x400-m relay	1st place; 3:22.62 minutes
2004	Athens, Greece	Shelia Burrell	Heptathlon	4th place; 6296 points
		Hazel Clark	800-m run	Did not qualify for finals; 2:05.67 minutes
		LaTasha Colander	100-m dash	8th place; 11.18 seconds
		Gail Devers	100-m dash	7th place in semis; 11.22 seconds
			100-m hurdles	Did not finish
		Allyson Felix	200-m dash	2nd place; 22.18 seconds
		Joanna Hayes	100-m hurdles	1st place; 12.37 seconds; Olympic Record
		Monique Hennagan	400-m run	3rd place; 49.97 seconds
		Tiombe Hurd	Triple Jump	Did not qualify for finals; 45' 10 ½"

Year	Location	Athlete	Event	Performance
2004	Athens, Greece	Sheena Johnson	400-m hurdles	4th place; 53.83 seconds
		Marion Jones	Long jump	5th place; 6.85 meters
		Muna Lee	200-m dash	7th place; 22.87 seconds
		Jearl Miles-Clark	800-m run	6th place; 1:57.27 minutes
		Melissa Morrison	100-m hurdles	3rd place; 12.56 seconds
		Sanya Richards	400-m run	5th place; 50.19 seconds
		Brenda Taylor	400-m hurdles	7th place; 54.97 seconds
		DeeDee Trotter	400-m run	4th place; 50.00 seconds
		Angela Williams, Marion Jones, Lauryn Williams, LaTasha Colander	4x100-m relay	Did not finish
		DeeDee Trotter, Monique Henderson, Sanya Richards, Monique Hennagan	4x400-m relay	1st place; 3:19.01
2008	Beijing, China			

126

BIBLIOGRAPHY

BOOKS AND ARTICLES

Baker, William. *Jesse Owens: An American Life*. New York: The Free Press.

Biracree, Tom. *Wilma Rudolph: Champion Athlete*. New York: Chelsea House Publishers, 1988.

Cahn, Susan. *Coming on Strong: Gender and Sexuality in Twentieth-Century Women's Sport*. New York: The Free Press, 1994.

Cayleff, Susan. *Babe: The Life and Legend of Babe Didrikson Zaharias*. Urbana: University of Illinois Press, 1995.

Condon, Robert J. *Great Women Athletes of the 20th Century*. Jefferson, NC: McFarland, 1991.

Davis, Marianna W. (ed.). *Contributions of Black Women to America: Volume I*. Columbia, SC: Kenday Press, Inc., 1982.

Davis, Michael D. *Black American Women in Olympic Track and Field*. Jefferson, NC: McFarland & Company, Inc., 1992.

Gibson, Althea. *I Always Wanted to be Somebody*. New York: Harpercollins, 1958.

Lewis, Dwight and Susan Thomas. *A Will to Win*. Mt. Juliet, TN: Cumberland Press, 1983.

Liberti, Rita M. "'We Were Ladies, We Just Played Basketball Like Boys' African American Womanhood and Competitive Basketball at Bennett College, 1928–1942," *Journal of Sport History*, 26 (Fall 1999): 567–84.

Mandell, Richard D. *The Nazi Olympics*. Urbana: University of Illinois Press, 1987.

Oglesby, Carole A. "Myths and Realities of Black Women in Sport." In *Black Women in Sport,* ed. Tina Sloan Green. Reston, VA: AAHPERD Publications, 1981.

Robinson, Jackie. *I Never Had It Made.* New York: G.P. Putnam's Sons, 1971.

Rudolph, Wilma, with Martin Ralbovsky. *Wilma: The Story of Wilma Rudolph.* New York: Signet, 1977.

Ryan, Joan. *Contributions of Women: Sports.* Minneapolis, MN: Dillon Press, Inc., 1975.

Smith, Yevonne R. "Women of Color in Society and Sport," *Quest* (August 1992): 236–37.

Temple, Ed, with B'Lou Carter. *Only the Pure in Heart Survive.* Nashville, TN: Broadman Press, 1980.

Tygiel, Jules. *Baseball's Great Experiment: Jackie Robinson and His Legacy.* New York: Oxford University Press, 1983.

Wiggins, David K. (ed.). *African Americans in Sport: Volume 1.* Armonk, NY: M.E. Sharpe, 2004.

Wiggins, David K. (ed.). *African Americans in Sport: Volume 2.* Armonk, NY: M.E. Sharpe, 2004.

Wilson, Wayne. "Wilma Rudolph: The Making of an Olympic Icon." In *Sport and the Racial Mountain: A Biographical History of the African American Athlete,* ed. David K. Wiggins. Fayetteville: University of Arkansas Press, forthcoming.

Woolum, Janet. *Outstanding Women Athletes: Who They Are and How They Influenced Sports in America.* Phoenix, AZ: Oryx Press, 1992.

Young, A. S. "Doc." *Negro Firsts in Sports.* Chicago: Johnson Publishing Company Inc., 1963.

Zaharias, Babe Didrikson, as told to Harry Paxton. *This Life I've Led: My Autobiography.* New York: A.S. Barnes, 1955.

NEWSPAPERS AND MAGAZINES

Alfano, Peter. "3 Golds Change Little in Brisco-Hooks Life." *New York Times,* 25 January 1985, A19.

Ashford, Evelyn. "In her tracks." *New York Times,* 1 January 1995, SM37.

"Athlete in Protest." *New York Times,* 30 May 1963, 32.

"Athletes Honored for Perseverance." *New York Times,* 11 October 1991, B12.

Berkow, Ira. "Sports of the Times; Forever the Regal Champion." *New York Times,* 13 November 1994, S9.

Berkow, Ira. "Sports of the Times; Years Later, Jones feels a link to Owens." *New York Times,* 9 February 2001.

Brody, Tom C. "At Last the Girls Are Ours." *Sports Illustrated,* 17 August 1964, 68.

Danzig, Allison. "Norton Runs out of Passing Zone." *New York Times*, 9 September 1960, 20.

"Ex-Olympian On SSC Staff." *Sacramento Union*, 1 October 1970, B1.

"The Fastest Female." *Time*, 19 September 1960, 74–75.

Friendly, Jr., Alfred. "Wilma Rudolph Denies Selling Medals." *New York Times*, 26 March 1969, 54.

Gerald, Zenobia Jonell. "Rudolph's Free to Run a Winning Streak." *Sacramento Bee*, 2 June 1981, B4.

"Girl on the Run." *Newsweek*, 6 February 1961, 54.

Hackett, Thomas. "Speed Demon." *New York Times*, 14 May 2000.

Heilman, Barbara. "Like Nothing Else in Tennessee." *Sports Illustrated*, 14 November 1960, 50.

Lipsyte, Robert M. "Wilma Rudolph Pauses Briefly for Medal, Visit and Plaudits." *New York Times*, 27 September 1960, 46.

Litsky, Frank. "Griffith Joyner Wins More than Gold." *New York Times*, 30 September 1988, A16.

Litsky, Frank. "Wilma Rudolph, Star of the 1960 Olympics, Dies at 54." *New York Times*, 13 November 1994, 53.

Longman, Jere. "How the Women Won." *New York Times*, 23 June 1996.

Lovett, Bobby. "Leaders of Afro-American Nashville: Wilma Rudolph and the TSU Tigerbelles." 1997 Nashville Conference on Afro-American Culture and History.

Maule, Tex. "U.S. and U.S.S.R. About-Face." *Sports Illustrated*, 16 July 1962, 18–19, 54.

Maule, Tex. "Whirling Success for the U.S." *Sports Illustrated*, 30 July 1962, 14.

"Miss Rudolph heads Track team for '62." *New York Times*, 13 December 1962, 14.

"Miss Rudolph's Coach Dies." *New York Times*, 10 April 1963, 22.

"Mrs. Ward Captures Dash." *New York Times*, 29 August 1962, 43.

Murray, James. "A Big Night for Wilma." *Sports Illustrated*, 30 January 1961, 48.

"Pope Honors Miss Rudolph." *New York Times*, 27 May 1969, 57.

"President is host to Wilma Rudolph." *New York Times*, 15 April 1961, 12.

Rhoden, William C. "The End of a Winding Road." *New York Times*, 19 November 1994, 31.

Roberts, M. B. "Rudolph ran and world went wild." http://espn.go.com/sportscentury/features/00016444.html (accessed 18 December 2005).

Schwartz, Larry. "Her Roman Conquest." http://espn.go.com/sportscentury/features/00016446.html (accessed 18 December 2005).

Scoreboard. *Sports Illustrated*, 3 September 1956, 40–41.

"She Runs in Mother's Footsteps." *New York Times*, 8 April 1973, 259.

Snow, Mary. "Can the Soviet Girls Be Stopped?" *Sports Illustrated*, 27 August 1956, 10–11.

"Storming the Citadel." *Time*, 10 February 1961, 57.

Teague, Robert D. "Everyone has Wilma on the Run." *New York Times*, 4 February 1961, 11.

"Tennessee A. and I. Women Gain National Indoor Track Crown." *New York Times*, 25 January 1959, S1.

"Tennessee State Honors Coach with a New Track." *New York Times*, 9 April 1978, S4.

Underwood, John. "This is the Way the Girls Go." *Sports Illustrated*, 10 May 1965, 45.

Verschoth, Anita. "Some Dashing Dolls Debut in Dayton." *Sports Illustrated*, 14 July 1969, 20.

"Wilma Rudolph Graduates." *New York Times*, 28 May 1963, 61.

"Wilma Rudolph Lends Grace to Reunion." *New York Times*, 28 March 1976, 170.

"Wilma Rudolph Married." *New York Times*, 29 November 1961, 50.

"Wilma Rudolph Repeats as Top Female Athlete." *New York Times*, 19 December 1961, 45.

"Wilma Rudolph Sets 2 Records." *New York Times*, 17 April 1960, S7.

"World Speed Queen." *New York Times*, 9 September 1960, 20.

FILMS

Wilma (1977). New York: Cappy Productions.

Wilma Rudolph: Olympic Champion [film] (1961). U.S. Information Agency. Available from Archives II, Record Group 306.5247.

INDEX

1932 Olympic Games, Los Angeles, 31, 32, 98

1936 Olympic Games, Berlin, 32, 107

1948 Olympic Games, London, 23, 31, 33, 34

1952 Olympic Games, Helsinki, 23, 24, 52

1956 Olympics Games, Melbourne, 17, 34, 37, 38, 48, 52, 80, 100; preparation for, 32, 33, 35, 36; trials, 23–25

1960 Olympic Games, Rome, 38, 47, 60, 61, 79, 80, 100, 103, 104, 109; Coach Temple and, 52, 57; European tour following, 62, 63, 65; medal count, 60; preparation for, 53, 54, 56, 57; press coverage of, 61, 62, 69; television coverage of, 56, 57; trials, 53; Wilma's gold medal events at, 58, 59, 77, 79, 80, 103

1964 Olympic Games, Tokyo, 16, 70, 85, 86

1968 Olympic Games, Mexico City, 88

1972 Olympic Games, Munich, 104

1976 Olympic Games, Montreal, 104, 106

1984 Olympic Games, Los Angeles, 91, 106

1988 Olympic Games, Seoul, 106, 107

2000 Olympic Games, Sydney, 107, 108

2004 U.S. Track and Field Olympic Trials, 105

Abbott, Cleveland, 11, 12, 16, 17, 33

Abbott, Jessie, 16

Abdul-Jabbar, Kareem, 104

Africa, 72, 73

African American women in sport, track and field, 29, 33, 34, 48–50, 53, 55, 61, 62,105

Albany, Georgia, 34

Ali, Muhammad, 61, 91, 104

Allison, Mrs., 3, 12

Amateur Athletic Union (AAU), 109, 110; 1954 outdoor meet, 35; 1955 outdoor meet, 18, 20, 24, 35, 96; 1956 outdoor meet, 21–23, 35, 96; 1957 outdoor meet, 43, 48; 1959 indoor meet, 49, 52; 1959 outdoor meet, 52; 1960 indoor meet, 52; 1960 outdoor meet, 53; 1961 outdoor meet, 70; 1962 outdoor meet, 70; All-American awards, 72; integration of, 11, 20; Tuskegee dominance of, 11, 12

Amateurism, 64, 68, 70, 71, 108

Amsterdam, Holland, 62

Anderson, Annette, 21

Anderson, Marian, 79

Armstrong-Perkins, Marion, 18, 34, 35, 51, 70

Ashford, Evelyn, 103, 104, 106

Associated Press Award, 64, 70, 71

Athens, Greece, 49, 62

Atlanta, 35, 64

Atlanta Daily World, 34

Baltimore, Maryland, 86

Baptist Christian Athletes, 73

Basilica of Maxentius, 56

Bayshore, New York, 23

Belafonte, Harry, 65

Berkow, Ira, 110

Berlin, Germany, 32, 62, 107

Bethune Cookman College, 34

Betty Crocker Award, 65

Black Sports Hall of Fame, 104

Blankers-Koen, Fanny, 23

Blanton, Ray, 90

Booker T. Washington High School, 33, 52

Boston, Ralph, 80, 83, 86, 87

Bowen, Nancy, 10, 41, 43

Brennen, John, 23

Brentwood, Tennessee, 91

Brisco Hooks, Valerie, 104, 106

British Empire Games, 62, 63

Brown, Barbara, 68

Brown, Earlene, 60

Brown, Jim, 73, 96

Brown, Vivian, 68–70

Brown v. Board of Education (1954), 3, 78

Budapest, Hungary, 49

Buffalo, New York, 23

Bunche, Ralph, 79

Burt High School, 9, 11, 20, 43, 44, 47, 63; basketball team, 7–11, 13, 15, 38, 41, 42; prom, 42, 43; track team, 9–12, 42; welcome home celebration, 38, 41, 63, 64

Cahn, Susan, 29, 30, 49, 61

California State University, Northridge, 106

Carew, Mary, 32

Carlos, John, 88

Catholic Youth Organization, 52

Chamberlain, Wilt, 73, 96

Charleston, West Virginia, 90

Chicago, 30, 32, 52, 69, 86, 88, 89

Chicago Comets, 20

Chicago Defender, 31, 32

Christopher Columbus Award, 64

Clarksville, Tennessee, 25, 36, 38, 41–43, 48, 104, 105, 109; First Baptist Church, 92; *Leaf-Chronicle*, 59; segregation, 1–5, 73, 97; welcome home celebration, 59, 63–65, 81, 97

Clay, Cassius. *See* Muhammad Ali
Cleveland, Ohio, 43, 86
Clinton, Bill, 104
Coachman, Alice, 23, 33, 34
Cobb Elementary School, 3, 5, 85, 86
Cold War, 29, 30, 38, 49, 57, 77, 83
Coleman, Dr., 1–2
Cologne, Germany, 62
Corpus Christi, Texas, 53
Cowan, Rus, 32
Craig, Leroy, 16
Crowder, Shirley, 42, 52, 60
Crown Royal Achievement Award, 104
Cuthbert, Betty, 36, 37

Dakar, Senegal, 72
Daley, Richard, 64; Youth Foundation, 69, 71, 89, 90
Daniels, Isabelle, 23–25, 30, 34, 49, 51; background, 35; Olympic performances, 37
Davis, Walter, 16, 80
DeFrantz, Anita, 103
de Hoog, Walter, 82
Delta Sigma Theta, 65
DePauw University, 91
Detroit, Michigan, 64, 86, 87
deVarona, Donna, 86
Devers, Gail, 104
Didrikson Zaharias, Babe, 32, 65, 72, 98, 99
Distinguished American Series, 105

Ebony, 49, 88, 91, 106
"Ed Sullivan Show", 64
Eldridge, Djuana, 86

Eldridge, Robert, 8, 64, 97, 100; dating Wilma, 11, 19, 42, 43, 47, 70; marriage to Wilma, 71, 73, 85, 86, 89; divorce from Wilma, 90, 91
Eldridge, Robert, Jr., 86
Eldridge, Xurry, 89
Eldridge, Yolanda, 43, 44, 47, 63, 71, 74, 82, 86, 89, 90
Ellington, Buford, 16, 59, 63, 65
Emporia, Kansas, 53
Emporia State College, 53
ESPN, 104
Evansville, Indiana, 86

Faggs, Mae, 19, 30, 34, 35, 52, 72, 110; accomplishments, 38; background, 23; leadership, 23–25, 32, 33, 36, 59; Olympic performances, 23, 24, 37
Femininity, 68, 108; American views on female athletes and, 73, 105; Black community's views of, 8, 31, 44, 48–51, 73; press coverage of, 61, 62, 68, 72, 106, 107; Soviet women and, 30, 48, 72
Fiji Islands, 36
Fisk University, 2
Fletcher, Ruth, 10
Florida A&M, 35
Frankfurt, Germany, 62
Franklin Field, 21

Games of Friendship, 72
Gary, Indiana, 70
General Mills, 69
Gibson, Althea, 55, 64, 77, 79
Graham, Billy, 73
Gray, Clinton, 11, 12, 13, 42, 96; basketball season, 7–10,

38, 43; death of, 73, 85; track
   season, 9,10
Greensboro, North Carolina, 78
Greenspan, Bud, 90, 100, 110
Greenwood, Mississippi, 35
Griffith-Joyner, Florence, 104,
   106, 107

Hard, Darlene, 70
Hardy, Catherine, 24
Harris, Tom, 17
Harrisburg, Pennsylvania, 15, 35
Hawaii, 36
Heine, Jutta, 58
Helms World Trophy, 64
Helsinki, Finland, 23
Henderson, Edwin B., 8, 33
Hopkinsville, Kentucky, 42
Horne, Lena, 65
Hudson, Martha, 20, 21, 35, 49;
   background, 19; Olympic per-
   formances, 59, 60
Humphrey, Hubert, 86
Hyman, Dorothy, 58

Il Tempo, 88
Indianapolis, Indiana, 91
International Olympic
   Committee (IOC), 30, 58

Jackson, Marion E., 34
Jackson, Nell, 23, 33
James E. Sullivan Award, 64, 70
Jet, 85, 86, 106
Jim Crow, 2, 5
Job Corps Center, 86, 87
John Harris High School, 15
Johnson, Lyndon, 69, 81
Johnson, Rafer, 61, 64, 79
Jones, Barbara, 24, 30, 49, 52, 53;
   Olympic performances, 59, 60

Jones, Marion, 104, 107, 108
Joyner-Kersee, Jackie, 104, 107

Kansas State University, 53
Kennedy, John F., 69, 81
Kersee, Bob, 107
King, Billie Jean, 104
King, Martin Luther, Jr., 78, 87

Lacy, Sam, 91
Ladies Professional Golf
   Association (LPGA), 55, 98
Leone, Giuseppina, 58
Life, 106
Linden, New Jersey, 70
Little Rock, Arkansas, 78
Logan, Bobby, 69
London, England, 23, 62
Lopiano, Donna, 107, 108
Los Angeles, 32, 33, 35, 53, 86,
   87, 91, 98, 105
Los Angeles Times, 64;
   Invitational, 67, 68, 72
Louis, Joe, 106
Louisville, Kentucky, 69

Macon County Training School,
   60
Mademoiselle, 64
Madison Square Garden, 68
Manuel, Theresa, 34
Marshall, Pappy, 19
Mason-Dixie Games, 69
Mathews, Margaret, 23, 25;
   background, 34; Olympic per-
   formances, 37, 49, 51
Mattson, Ollie, 86
Mays, Willie, 73
McDaniel, Mildred, 35, 37
McGuire, Edith, 70, 73, 103, 106
McNabb, Mary, 35

McRae, Georgia, 19
Meharry Hospital, 2–5
Melbourne, Australia, 17, 25, 36, 56, 80, 109
Merry High School, 42
Millrose Games, 67, 68
Moreau, Janet, 24
Moscow, 49, 70
Murray, Jim, 67, 68

Nashville, Tennessee, 2, 13, 25, 41, 87; Baptist Hospital, 91; girls high school basketball championships, 11, 41; *Nashville Banner*, 65; Tennessee State University, 17, 18, 31, 43, 47, 63, 80
National Association for the Advancement of Colored People (NAACP), 64
National Collegiate Athletic Association (NCAA), 104
National Sports Award, 104
National Woman's Hall of Fame, 104
Newark, New Jersey, 86
Newcombe, Don, 22
Newsweek, 68, 106
New York Athletic Club, 67, 69
New York City, 56, 61, 68, 69
New York Times, 65, 88, 110
Norton, Ray, 58, 61, 68, 97

Olympic Village, 36, 56, 57, 60
Operation Champ, 86, 87
Oriard, Michael, 95, 96, 99
Oslo, Norway, 72
Owens, Jesse, 99, 106, 107, 110

Paese Sera, 87
Palmer, Arnold, 104

Palo Alto, California, 71, 72
Pan American Games, 31, 35, 44, 49, 52, 53
Parks, Rosa, 78
Patterson, Audrey, 23
Patterson, Floyd, 96
Pearl High School, 11
Pelham Junior High School, 87
Penn Relays, 21, 67
Pennsylvania State University, 16
Petty, Wilbert C., 72
Philadelphia, Pennsylvania, 21–23, 25, 53, 64, 96, 100
Pickett, Tidye, 31, 32
Playdays, 9
Poland Springs, Maine, 86
Police Athletic League, 23, 52, 71
Polio, 1, 2, 104, 109
Pollard, Ernestine, 70
Ponca City, Oklahoma, 18, 20, 24, 25, 96
Pope John XXIII, 62
Pope Paul VI, 88
Press, Irina, 59
Press coverage, 31, 55, 61, 62, 67, 68, 105, 106, 108
Providence, Rhode Island, 23, 33

Queen Mercurettes, 52

Ralbovsky, Martin, 95
Riggs, Bobby, 104
Riots, 86
Roba, Alabama, 60
Robinson, Jackie, 22, 23, 77
Rodgers, Neomia, 60
Roman Coliseum, 56
Rome, Italy, 54, 56, 59, 70, 79, 80
Rudolph, Blanche, 1–4, 7, 13, 18, 43, 44, 47, 61, 63, 64, 69, 81, 100

Rudolph, Charlene, 53, 81, 87
Rudolph, Ed, 1, 4, 5, 7, 13, 18,
    43, 44, 47, 63, 81, 100
Rudolph, Wilma: AAU meets,
    20–22, 24, 69, 70; attending
    Tennessee State University, 47–
    53, 65, 83; awards, 64, 65, 104,
    105; children, 43,44, 47, 63, 71,
    74, 82, 83, 86, 89, 90; child-
    hood, 1–6; death, 91, 92, 104,
    109, 110; employment, 85, 86,
    87, 90, 91; film, 100, 101; high
    school basketball, 7–11, 13, 41,
    42; high school track, 9, 10, 12;
    illnesses and injuries, 1–3, 52,
    57, 82; loneliness, 3, 5; mar-
    riages, 70, 71, 73, 83, 85, 86, 97;
    meeting Jackie Robinson, 22,
    23; meeting President John F.
    Kennedy, 69; Olympic perfor-
    mances, 36–38, 56–60; Olympic
    trials, 25, 53, 54; pregnancy, 43,
    44, 47, 50, 83, 86; preparation
    for the Olympics, 33–35; reli-
    gion, 5, 43, 62, 73, 81; retire-
    ment, 71–73, 83; siblings, 1–5,
    7, 8, 19, 43, 47, 53, 81, 87; sum-
    mer program at Tennessee State
    University, 17–19, 21, 43, 44;
    thoughts on race and racism,
    2, 4, 5, 36, 83, 88, 97, 98; trip
    to Africa, 72–73; USIA film,
    79–83; writing her autobiogra-
    phy, 95–101
Rudolph, Wesley, 4, 5
Rudolph, Yvonne, 7, 8, 43, 47
Russell, Bill, 73, 87, 96

Sacramento State College, 88, 89
Salk, Jonas, 2
Schwenk, Melinda, 79, 80, 82, 96

Silver Anniversary Award, 104
Smith, Annie Lois, 49
Smith, Tommie, 88
Snow, Mary, 31
South Africa, 56
Soviet Union: Cold War politics,
    77, 78, 83; Olympic team, 23,
    37, 59, 60; sporting rivalry
    with U.S., 29–31, 44, 52, 53,
    71, 72, 105
Sports Illustrated, 31, 34, 71–73,
    105
Sports Magazine Award, 65
Stadio Olympico, 58, 59
St. Bethlehem, Tennessee, 1
Stephens, Helen, 32, 57
St. Louis, Missouri, 47, 87
Stokes, Louise, 31, 32
Stuttgart, Germany, 70
Sundquist, Don, 104

Temple, Charlie, 16
Temple, Christopher, 15
Temple, Ed, 33, 37, 47, 65, 69, 70,
    71, 80, 85, 90, 100, 105, 109;
    coaching Olympic teams, 52,
    53, 57, 58, 59; coaching Pan-
    Am Games, 49, 52; education
    of, 15, 16; hiring at TSU, 16;
    philosophies of coaching, 17,
    22, 44, 48–50, 57; philosophies
    of femininity, 48–51, 61, 62,
    68, 69; summer program at
    Tennessee State University, 13,
    18, 19, 21, 23, 43
Temple, Edwina, 16
Temple, Georgia, 52
Temple, Lloyd Bernard, 16
Temple, Ruth, 15
Tennessee Department of
    Economic Development, 90

Tennessee High School Girls Championships, 11

Tennessee State University, 13, 20, 21, 29, 47, 70, 91, 103; athletic tradition of, 73; dominance of women's track team, 29; Hall of Fame, 91; history of, 24, 48; summer track program, 13, 17, 19, 21, 41, 43, 44, 51, 52; USIA film, 80, 82

Terme di Caracella, 56

Terry, Jo Ann, 70

Texas Christian University, 53

Thompson, Cynthia, 24, 35

Till, Emmett, 78

Time, 58, 62, 106

Title IX, 90

Torrance, Gwen, 104, 107

Truman, Harry, 34

Tuskegee Institute, 35; relays, 11, 12, 19, 24, 96; summer program, 13, 60; track team, 16, 17, 33, 34

Tyson, Cicely, 90, 100

Tyus, Wyomia, 73, 103, 106

Underwood, John, 73

United States Information Agency (USIA), 78, 79, 82, 83, 97

United States Olympic Committee (USOC), 32

United States Olympic Hall of Fame, 104

United States Postal Service, 105

United States State Department, 72

United States Track and Field Hall of Fame, 104

University of California Los Angeles, 22, 88

University of Pennsylvania, 21

University of Southern California, 33

U.S. Open, 55

Verschoth, Anita, 105

Walker, Mabel, 34

Ward, William, 70, 71, 83, 97

Warsaw, Poland, 49

Washington, Booker T., 5

Washington, DC, 35, 52, 64, 69, 86

Washington, Denzel, 100

Watts Community Action Committee, 87

Welch, Fran, 53

West Germany, 58, 59, 70, 89

White, Mildred, 60

White, Willye, 21, 23; background, 35, Olympic performances, 38, 49, 60, 70; thoughts on femininity, 51

Williams, Lucinda, 20, 23, 24, 35, 49, 51, 53, 56; Olympic performances, 59, 60, 62

Williams, Ted, 104

Wilma Rudolph Foundation, 91, 109

Wilma Unlimited, 90, 91

Wimbledon, 55, 77, 79

Women's Sports Foundation, 107

Woods, Tiger, 108

World War II, 5, 33

Wright, Mickey, 70

Wright, Stan, 88, 89

Wuppertal, Germany, 62

Young, A. S. "Doc", 73

Young, Fay, 31

About the Author

MAUREEN M. SMITH is a Professor at California State University, Sacramento in the Department of Kinesiology and Health Science.